T0158990

MY LIFE
ON THE
COURTS

Henry H. Kennedy Jr.

MY LIFE ON THE COURTS

iUniverse books may be ordered through booksellers or by contacting:

iUniverse
1663 Liberty Drive
Bloomington, IN 47403
www.iuniverse.com
1-800-Authors (1-800-288-4677)

Because of the dynamic nature of the Internet, any web addresses or links contained in this book may have changed since publication and may no longer be valid. The views expressed in this work are solely those of the author and do not necessarily reflect the views of the publisher, and the publisher hereby disclaims any responsibility for them.

Any people depicted in stock imagery provided by Getty Images are models, and such images are being used for illustrative purposes only.
Certain stock imagery © Getty Images.

ISBN: 978-1-5320-6372-5 (sc)
ISBN: 978-1-5320-6374-9 (hc)
ISBN: 978-1-5320-6373-2 (e)

Library of Congress Control Number: 2018915118

Print information available on the last page.

iUniverse rev. date: 04/24/2019

To my mother and father, Rachel Spann Kennedy and Henry H. Kennedy Sr.; my wife, Altomease Rucker; and my daughters, Morgan and Alexandra.

INTRODUCTION

The primary impetus for this memoir was the urging of my psychiatrists who pressed me to reflect on and write about my life for therapeutic reasons as a treatment for depression. I resisted because I had little energy to do anything and felt that I had little worthwhile to write about. I told them that I would not want to waste time on something as insignificant as musings about my life. My last psychiatrist, Dr. Kevin Williams, persisted, however, saying that only he and I would read it. After all, I would not be wasting my time, as the writing of it would have significant therapeutic benefits for me, and I would not be wasting his time, as I would pay him to read it.

As it turns out, several years passed before I embarked on a most gratifying journey, Purposefully looking back in time I have recalled the people and events that have shaped, added texture, and meaning to my life. I have come to believe that there are those who will find something of interest in reading about my experiences, thoughts, and feelings over the course of my lifetime, many of them having to do with courts—courts of law and tennis courts.

I hope those who experience clinical depression, as I did for many years, will draw inspiration from my story of having survived the hell of depression and then thriving more than ever. I sunk as low as can be, but with treatment by skilled professionals, faith that I could get better, and, crucially, my willingness to accept and embrace the support of loved ones, I have been able to completely reclaim my life and make it even better than before. Those who are similarly afflicted can do the same, I believe, by following the same template.

Most of us when remembering the distant past look backward through rose-colored lenses, a tint that sometimes alters our perceptions about the events we are recalling but almost always significantly distorts how we felt at the time of those events. For those suffering with depression, there is an additional phenomenon at play. Dr. Williams notes, "Depression will try to steal all but your most troubling memories."

I have endeavored to adjust for these shadings so that I describe past events accurately and accomplish the more difficult challenge: to recall my feelings and thoughts as they occurred and then to express them, with all their complexity and nuance, in the present as if in real time.

The bottom line is this: While there have been lows in my life to be sure, they are overwhelmingly outnumbered by the highs. I have come to embrace this realization. And, just as my psychiatrists predicted, recalling and writing about these peaks and valleys by some unknown process have been incalculably beneficial for my emotional and mental well-being.

My current state of contentment is due in large part to the generosity and compassion of the many fine people with whom I have had the good fortune to come into contact over the years. Many of these people I write about in this memoir, others I mention only in the acknowledgments that follow the main body of this writing, and some I have not mentioned at all, but as is often snidely said but done so respectfully and sincerely here: You know who you are.

1 CHAPTER
MENTAL ILLNESS

In 1982, when I was thirty-two years old and a judge on the Superior Court of the District of Columbia, I was diagnosed with a serious mental illness, one that carries an Axis I designation in the *Diagnostic and Statistical Manual of Mental Disorders*, major depressive disorder, recurrent. My depression was mostly endogenous, which means that it most often originated from within, rather than exogenous, a condition in which symptoms are activated by an outside source, like, for example, the loss of a job or the death of a loved one.

I use the past tense because it has been seven years since I have had any symptoms of depression and I am confident that I have emerged from this affliction for good.

Whereas there were times when I took as many as four antidepressant medications at the same time and engaged in talk therapy at least once a week, I now take only one antidepressant medication, Trazadone, that is principally prescribed to assist me with my difficulty in remaining asleep for a period of time necessary for good overall health, and I am no longer in therapy. It is ironic that my dog, a two-year old Tibetan Terrier named Princeton, has also been prescribed trazadone, as needed, to calm him.

The symptoms of my illness emerged periodically, sometimes but not always, when I was faced with what I considered to be an important and substantial challenge, one that I might not be able to successfully meet even if I had theretofore successfully met a similar challenge. Such a scenario presented a circumstance in which I might fail, a risk to my psyche that if realized would strike at my very core.

I had classic symptoms, unremitting fatigue, difficulty concentrating, extreme unexplained sadness, thought deprivation, and self-loathing. I never attempted suicide, but I often cogitated that it would be better for all concerned if I were dead. I hoped for an accident that would quickly and painlessly end my life. That way, I would be rid of the psychological pain but would be free from fault for committing a cowardly and shameful act.

When in the throes of an episode of depression, which would come on suddenly and last for months, until the last one, which lasted four years, everything—literally everything—was exceedingly difficult, from my struggling to express myself, orally and in writing, to making a decision about what to order to eat at a restaurant, and, sometimes, even getting out of bed in the morning and starting my day.

William Styron, the author of *The Confessions of Nat Turner*, among other notable works, quite aptly describes depression in his book *Darkness Visible*:

> Depression is a disorder of mood so mysteriously painful and elusive in the way it becomes known to the self—to the meditating intellect—that it is close to being beyond description. It thus remains nearly incomprehensible to those who have not experienced it in its extreme mode, although the gloom, the blues that people go through occasionally and associate with the general hassle of everyday existence are of such prevalence that they do give many individuals a hint of the illness in its catastrophic form.

As bothersome as the symptoms of depression were, equally burdensome were the substantial efforts I made to hide them from others to avoid the stigma that regrettably still comes with this disease. No matter how often my psychiatrists would equate mental illness with physical illness or I made such a comparison myself intellectually, in my heart, I felt that my infirmity was quite unlike a physical illness. Rather, my malady was "my fault," one that was rooted in and evidenced a profound character flaw that a "better" person would not have.

This attitude fed into and exacerbated the self-loathing and shame that are hallmarks of the disease and are perhaps the most damaging and dangerous of its several symptoms. It is these symptoms that tragically, all too often, lead the depressed person to end the searing psychological pain by taking his or her own life.

My descent into depression was, and still is, puzzling. Until my diagnosis at age thirty-two, I had not experienced any symptoms of the illness, though by that time I had experienced many circumstances that one might reasonably think would have resulted in a clinical mood disorder.

At an early age, I encountered rabid racism. I am short and dark skinned. Racial inferiority was an ever-present notion to be confronted.

Too, my father, whose approval I craved, put enormous pressure on me to excel at a time when it was far from certain whether I would be able to meet his lofty expectations.

When I was nine years old, my parents felt compelled to move to an unfamiliar city because of racial oppression and hostility, a motivation of which I was aware. It was in an unfamiliar city where I first attended integrated schools.

Consider too the challenges presented by my attending Princeton University, one of this country's elite universities. I, a person with a significant inferiority complex already, was well aware that I was admitted as a result of affirmative action and was not nearly as well equipped to face Princeton's rigorous academic requirements as most of my classmates, many of whom had "prepared" at exclusive schools like Groton, Lawrenceville, Andover, and Phillips Exeter or top-notch public schools that habitually send their graduates to elite colleges and universities. I did not feel that I deserved to be at this wonderful place.

After attending Harvard Law School, a school that then prided itself in its anxiety-producing Socratic teaching method, I was appointed a United States Magistrate when I was twenty-eight years old, the youngest federal judicial officer ever appointed. During my time as a United States Magistrate, I handled many extremely weighty and contentious proceedings for which I was ill prepared.

I suffered a short, failed marriage during which my former wife, Deloris Foskey, called me "spineless" because I would not buy a house I did not think we could afford but that she thought we could were we to employ a stratagem that required my parents to loan us money and provide a "gift letter."

Still, no sign of depression.

I first fell into depression when I was preparing to lead a discussion at a judges' prayer breakfast. The monthly breakfast meetings were organized by Judge Oliver Gasch, a United States district judge for the District of Columbia and a graduate of Princeton University. Judge Gasch was largely responsible for my first judicial appointment. The ecumenical breakfasts were attended by judges and justices on area courts monthly at the United States Capitol.

Ten to fifteen judges were typically in attendance and often included one or two Supreme Court justices. Antonin Scalia and Harry Blackmun attended more often than any of the other justices. The breakfasts tended to be very uplifting events. Typically, a meal of eggs, grits, and bacon was followed by a presentation by one of the judges or a guest speaker.

The presentation was followed by "highbrow" discussion of the presentation and of any issues it might implicate. For example, if the presenter talked about a vacation or conference in a foreign country, there might be discussion of the foreign policy of the United States with respect to that country. If the presentation concerned a judge's trip that included fly-fishing in Montana, the discussion might turn to the proper balance between protecting this country's natural resources and allowing for needed development and the extraction of those resources.

When Judge Gasch asked me to make a presentation, I naturally responded that I would. Of course, I wanted to do well, especially given my impressive audience. Also, Judge Gasch was a good friend of Dean Ernest Gordon, the former dean of the chapel at Princeton University who sometimes attended the breakfasts and had been instrumental in starting them. I had come to know and greatly respect him while I was a student at Princeton and had maintained contact with him following my graduation. .

The subject of my presentation was the most consequential trial in human history, the trial of Jesus Christ. More specifically, I talked about Jesus's second trial, as biblical historians pretty much agree that Jesus was subjected to two trials. The first was before the Supreme Sanhedrin, the central judicial body of the Jews in Judea in postexilic times, and the second a proceeding before Pontius Pilate, the Roman governor. The inspiration for this subject was a question my brother had posed to me after church one Sunday. He asked, "Why was Jesus crucified?" I, a judge and a Christian, quickly realized that I could come up with only the most general sort of answer.

Consulting a variety of sources, I was able to identify the most reasonable possibilities. I say possibilities because in assessing the trial of Jesus, one can hardly speak with certitude because all we have is a record created by persons who were absent from the events they wrote about and separated by time and geography from anyone who may have been present at the proceedings.

I thoroughly researched my subject and carefully prepared my remarks. My presentation was very well received by each attendee except for Justice Scalia. During the discussion that followed my presentation, he found nothing to explicitly criticize, but he took a totally unnecessary and altogether silly swipe at me for referencing the Swiss Catholic priest, theologian, and author Hans Kung. I cited Kung's book *On Being a Christian*, a work in which Kung affirms the vitality of Christianity by tracing it back to its roots and the reality of the historical Christ. It is not clear why Scalia, who claimed to be a devout Catholic, was critical of my citing Kung, as his remarks about Kung were purely ad hominem and not about any specific idea or thought by Kung that I referenced. It may be that Scalia's criticism was grounded on Kung's rejection of the Catholic doctrine of papal infallibility. Therefore, I speculate that Scalia felt that Kung was a heretic and, thus, not worthy of being favorably cited for any reason.

My short and infrequent contacts with Justice Scalia at these breakfasts where generosity of spirit was a virtue often referred to and displayed left me with the impression that he was anything but. To the contrary, Scalia had an illiberal and niggardly quality about him and evidenced a characteristic I dislike most in many of those who consider themselves religiously devout: the self-righteous refusal to countenance the proposition that they simply may be wrong about anything and certainly about what their religion calls its adherents to think and do.

Justice Harry Blackmun was exactly the opposite. Blackmun was humble, had a charitable disposition, and appeared authentically imbued with the Christian spirit. He also was a deep thinker who, unlike Justice Scalia, did not flaunt his considerable intelligence at every opportunity to do so.

After being diagnosed with mental illness, I was able to do my work as a judge even though I was periodically in depression's unrelenting grip. There were times when the disease caused me to falter, however. One time was when I was a judge on the DC Superior Court and was conducting a criminal plea proceeding, something I had done often and quite easily for years. I suddenly had difficulty speaking and panicked when I had difficulty remembering the routinized plea colloquy with the defendant that the taking of a criminal plea requires. My good friend and colleague, Judge Harriett Taylor, became aware of my having a break down, had my courtroom clerk call a recess, and then called a taxi and accompanied me to my psychiatrist on an emergency basis.

After this incident, my mother and brother came to our house at the request of my wife, Altomease ("Al"), to discuss whether I should be hospitalized, something I secretly desired as my despair at that point had reached an all-time low. Their collective judgment, however, held most strongly by Al, was that hospitalization was not immediately called for and only should be considered as a last resort.

Al was more concerned than anyone else, including me, about what hospitalization would mean for my career. As it turns out, for the ensuing years, I would soldier on as judge, husband, and father, engage in talk therapy as often as twice a week, and take different medication cocktails through periods of deep depression.

My first therapist was Dr. Allyce Gullattee, the mother of a high school classmate, to whom I was recommended by another psychiatrist based in Massachusetts, Dr. Alvin Poussaint, who my good friend Robert O'Meally had contacted after I had confided in him about my illness.

Dr. Gullattee is a proponent of the treatment methods of Sigmund Freud. Weekly, I would go to her office at Howard University Hospital where, after her office was darkened, we would talk while I reclined completely prone on a comfortable chaise. Gullattee's talk therapy involved discussion with me about my childhood, starting with my earliest memories as a child. She was convinced that the origin of my depression was some suppressed psychological trauma suffered at an early age.

After several months of talk therapy with Gullattee, my symptoms subsided, and I ended my treatment with her. By the time I next descended into depression, I had met Dr. Howard Hoffman who headed the Psychiatric Institute. I met Howard and his wife at a dinner party at the country home of Martin and Mary Thaler in Howard County, Maryland. I had been introduced to Martin and Mary years earlier by the parents of my college girlfriend, Betsy Paull. Betsy's mother was a cousin of Martin's first wife.

After dinner, the three couples played a lively game of charades. It occurred to me that if I ever needed a psychiatrist thereafter, I would contact Howard as I was very impressed with his intelligence and manner. Thus, when I descended into another depressive episode not long after first meeting him, Al called him and set up an appointment.

After several months, I again rebounded and left Howard's treatment. Against his advice, I discontinued taking antidepressant medication as I always have had an aversion to taking any kind of drug. About two years later, I returned to treatment with Howard. He enlisted the assistance of Adam Lowy, a psychiatrist at the Psychiatric Institute who had graduated from Harvard Medical School and was a highly regarded expert in psychopharmacology.

Unlike Gullattee, Howard was not Freudian in the least. He eschewed detailed exploration of my background and history and concentrated on talking with me about my present day-to-day concerns.

After my third or fourth depressive episode, I began to be treated by Lowy alone after Howard indicated that he had done all that he could for me. Later, I also started treatment with Kevin Williams, at the beginning, solely for concurrent talk therapy. Lowy discontinued his treatment of me when he learned that Williams, without consulting him, had prescribed medication for me. Williams prescribed the medication following a particularly despondent therapy session during which I expressed very dark thoughts regarding the prospect of my ever getting better. He worried that I might commit suicide and thought my condition warranted immediate additional anxiety medication.

Over the years that followed my presentation at the judges' prayer breakfast, I descended into depression seven more times. Each time, I was treated by psychiatrists almost all of whom urged me to write about my life. The therapist who was most insistent in this regard was Dr. Kevin Williams.

Williams had been recommended to Al by a friend whose child he had treated. Al sought out a black male psychiatrist as she felt that he perhaps would be better able to relate to me and understand some of the forces in my life that a white psychiatrist would not.

Williams, a graduate of Princeton University, in the class of 1983, and Yale Medical School, bleeds black and orange, Princeton's colors. He wears black and orange apparel in goofy combinations that are normally seen only on Princeton's campus and then only at reunions. He loves his association with Princeton and maintains his friendships with the people he met there, including Michelle Obama—whom he took to his Princeton senior prom. He also is friends with my sister, Angela Kennedy Acree, Michelle's classmate and roommate their sophomore year and next-door dorm neighbors in their junior and senior years. Dr. Williams continues his friendships with Michelle and Angela to this day.

Dr. Williams believed that writing a memoir would require me to reflect upon the many aspects of my life for which I should be proud and grateful. This, in turn, would fortify me to resist negative impulses and my tendency to glorify what I called "emotional authenticity," a view I expressed by saying, "I don't smile when I am not happy." This way of thinking ran directly counter to the instructions of my therapists who advised that I should "fake it till you make it." To do otherwise would be to submit to my grim feelings, feelings that at the same time were painful, sometimes excruciatingly so, yet peculiarly familiar and, therefore, in an odd way, relatively comfortable. The hope was that I might realize that I am not a disappointment or a failure, feelings that periodically infused my psyche for years, particularly when I was in the grip of depression.

Another person who urged me to write is Colbert King, a Pulitzer Prize–winning columnist for the *Washington Post*, a friend, and a fellow member of the DePriest 15, one of two social clubs to which I belong. Colby, who, as far as I know, was unaware of my depression, expressed that it would be important for me to write to memorialize my thoughts about the duties and responsibilities of my judicial offices and how I performed them. A superb writer himself, he said that my writing would be important for history's sake, particularly for the history of black people whose contributions are often overlooked because they are not documented. And, when they are, they are viewed through the unsympathetic lens of those who lack the perspective informed by the life experiences of a black person.

My intense fear of failing had a decided racial component and was a salient feature of my depression that led me to feel profound sadness for significant periods of time. As best I can describe it, the fear that gripped me for years was that while I had benefitted greatly from the sacrifices and struggles of others, much more than was my due, and had been the beneficiary of a superb education, I had not accomplished nearly enough to further the fortunes of others, particularly those of black people. The Old Testament teaching "[f]or everyone to whom much is given, from him much will be required" took root in my mind and lashed me psychologically whenever I felt that I had not measured up. I began to think that the collective judgment of my ancestors was perilously close to being one of condemnation of me for not doing my part to advance the race.

Doubtless, I had a totally unrealistic view of what I was duty bound to do. I thought frequently of the courage of the likes of the Reverend Martin Luther King Jr., Medgar Evers, Thurgood Marshall, and John Lewis, black men who set a standard by which I fell woefully short.

Equally worrisome was the fear that I had not sufficiently put to the lie a thought relegated to my subconscious at an early age, that I, and those of my race, are an inferior people.

The disabling symptoms of my depression, including my greatly diminished ability to concentrate and communicate, orally and in writing, loss of confidence, and perceived impaired judgment would not relent and caused me to retire on November 2, 2011.

In the months preceding my retirement, I interacted with Chief Judge Royce Lamberth much more than I previously had interacted with him or any other of the Chief Judges with whom I had served over the course of my time on the bench.

Ironically, shortly before I retired, Royce, a big Texas Republican, evidenced his confidence in my intellect and judgment by appointing me chair of the court's Rules Committee, the most important and demanding of the court's several committees. Thus, I was disappointed and knew that I would disappoint him when, given the toll my depression was taking on me and making it difficult for me keep up with my judicial duties, I stepped down as the head of the committee.

Thereafter, on three occasions, Al accompanied me to Royce's chambers and helped explain what I could and could not do. Royce always listened patiently and respectfully and was sensitive to the huge hit to my pride these conversations caused. During this time, Royce took on at least three extraordinarily difficult cases that I could not handle while also making timely decisions on other cases.

My visit to his chambers to tell him that I would step down was sad. I explained that despite my best efforts to address them, the symptoms of my depression were worsening and that I would have to undergo treatment that would keep me off the bench and out of the courthouse for an extended period of time. Royce was genuinely saddened, so much so that he teared up.

My family and I will always remember Royce's kindness and appreciate his display of character, which led him to graciously extend kindness and compassion to me at a crucial time without seeking any credit for doing so.

2 CHAPTER
MY FATHER

My unnatural fear of failing is traceable in large part to my relationship with my beloved father, Henry Harold Kennedy. That relationship is loving, supportive, and to a much lesser extent than when he was alive, demanding. I use the present tense because I still feel his love, support, and presence. While he exerted a tremendous amount of pressure on me in my early years and said things to me then that doubtless scarred me for life, he was always motivated by a profound love for me and desire that I succeed. But for Dad, I would not have accomplished anywhere near as much as I have, and I would not be living the wonderful life I live today.

My father

Dad had simple tastes and straightforward principles by which he lived. Paramount among these was the imperative that one protect and support his family in every way possible. He was true to this principle in small and big ways. For example, I doubt that any other student who attended Beauvoir and the National Cathedral School for girls, both upscale private schools, as did my sister Angela, had a parent who insisted on paying these schools' hefty fees in cash and personally would hand the money to the schools' treasurers. This was done primarily to demonstrate that Angela had "backup" and was to be treated fairly.

Another example is when Randy, my younger brother, won a Morehead scholarship in his senior year of high school, one that would have paid all of his tuition and fees as well to provide a stipend were he to attend the University of North Carolina for his baccalaureate degree as well for any graduate degree he were to pursue at that university. Randy, however, preferred to attend Princeton, which, while offering some financial aid, required a substantial contribution from my parents. Dad did not blink and financed Randy's education at Princeton.

Another example, seemingly insignificant but extremely consequential, was when I applied for admission to Princeton. On the way to the interview with two Princeton alumni who were to talk with me before submitting a report and recommendation on my application to Princeton's Dean of Admissions, Dad told me that during the interview I should develop an extreme "I" problem. That is, when answering any interviewer's question, I should convey self-confidence by referring to "I"—"I think this," "I did that," "I believe this," "I felt that," and so forth. I followed Dad's advice, and, as they say, the rest is history.

Years after the interview, I learned that it was scheduled to be done by three alumni but instead was conducted by two because the two interviewers managed to schedule the interview when the third could not attend because they knew that—regardless of the merits of how I performed—because I am black he would insist upon writing a negative report that would doom the chances of my being admitted.

One of my most vivid adolescent memories is of the challenge tennis match Dad set up between me and Edgar Lee, a DC firefighter in his late forties and a local tennis star. I was fourteen years old at the time. Dad had challenged Lee saying—among other things—that Lee was too old to beat me.

Dad had introduced me to tennis when I was eleven years old. For Christmas 1959, I had requested a Ping-Pong table as I had come to thoroughly enjoy the game that I learned and frequently played at the Takoma Recreation Center in Upper Northwest, Washington, DC.

Having an eleven-year-olds mind, in making my request, I gave no thought whatsoever to the fact that the small townhouse in which we lived at 730 Tewksbury Place, N.W. could not possibly accommodate a Ping-Pong table. Instead of a Ping-Pong table, Dad gave me a tennis racquet and a can of tennis balls, as it turns out, by far the most consequential gifts I have ever received.

Ironically, the gift of a tennis racquet was an outgrowth of Dad's disappointment that I had not performed well enough in the first sport in which I had competed, swimming. I had learned to swim when I was about five years old when we lived in Columbia, South Carolina, at a segregated pool not far from my maternal grandmother's home. I continued to swim when we moved to Washington where I was the captain and the only black member of the YMCA swim team.

During the three years I was on the team, I would attend morning practices, including those held during the winter months, by catching the J6 bus at Fifth and Van Buren Street. I would take the bus in the dark at six o'clock a.m. in order to get to the practices that started at seven. I would return home after practices, again by bus, in time to be at school by nine o'clock a.m.

My YMCA swim team

I did quite well in swim meets in DC, and when I was only twelve, I was good enough to train with the Howard University swim team.

However, I came in next to last in my best stroke, the breaststroke, in an important meet at the Northern Virginia Aquatic Club. In that competition in suburban northern Virginia, Olympic hopefuls were attempting to qualify for the US Olympic trials. A family friend, "Smitty" Smith, attempted to console me by saying, "Well, Henry, you got one!" No such words of consolation from Dad, however. Dad said the next day, "We need another sport." Hence, the gift of a tennis racquet the following Christmas.

Unbeknownst to my father, before issuing his challenge, Edgar Lee was a world-class athlete. He had been an accomplished runner and, while a college student at Virginia Union University, had won the mile and two-mile events at the Penn Relays as well as the CIAA championship in 1934.

In tennis competition, Edgar had beaten many of the very fine tennis players in the DC metropolitan area and nationally, many his junior, including Bobby Goeltz—the only person besides Arthur Ashe to win the National Interscholastic Championships three years in a row and Princeton's top singles player.

Edgar had been one of the first black men to play in the US Nationals held at the Westside Tennis Club in Forest Hills, New York, where, in 1954, he lost to the great Australian player Ken Rosewall. The same year he played the match against me arranged by my father he won the American Tennis Association's national championship, 45s singles division, as he did each year from 1957 to 1965, an unprecedented record that probably never will be broken.

The ATA was started by blacks in 1916 after the United States Lawn Tennis Association banned blacks from its tournaments. Egar was the ATA Men's 45 doubles champion in 1957-1958, 1960–65, 1967–68, 1973–74, and 1976. He also won the ATA Men's 55s singles title in 1972. He was inducted into the Virginia Union Hall of Fame in 1988 and the Mid-Atlantic Tennis Hall of Fame.

The challenge match with Edgar Lee was just two and a half years after I picked up a racquet for the first time. We played after school on a warm, sunny spring day on the red clay courts on the National Mall in the shadow of the Washington Monument.

Edgar, a man with an impressive dignified bearing, was very fleet afoot and hit his shots with unerring accuracy, especially his backhand. He was superbly conditioned and very wily. Several times, he hit deft drop shots to throw me off just when I was getting in a groove hitting my best shot, a hard topspin forehand. He also would pull me into the net to set me up for a high lob over my backhand side, thereby requiring me to try to hit the hardest shot in tennis, a backhand overhead. I do not remember the score, but it was not that close.

When the match was over, I was pleased that I had played as well as I had. I recognized that Edgar was a seasoned competitor with superior skills, an entirely different kettle of fish from the opponents I had played up to that point. Dad was anything but pleased, however, and he made no attempt to disguise his disappointment. He waited until we were no longer within hearing of Edgar and then spat, "You are a disgrace." The sentiment was unmistakably etched in his scowling face. During the unbearably long ride home, he told me this again and again while going over the different things I had done wrong and the mistakes I had made that led to my (our) defeat.

Not only had I been soundly defeated by Edgar, but because of Dad's reaction, I also felt humiliated and, even worse, that I had let him down.

As it turns out, Edgar came to like and respect me as a player and person, and he asked me several times to be his doubles partner in tournaments. We would drive to the tournaments accompanied by his wife of many years in his cream-colored Buick Electra 225, which was fully stocked with drinks we would consume during match play. Edgar's favorite was V8 vegetable juice. I was honored when he asked me to introduce him upon his induction into the USTA Mid-Atlantic Hall of Fame.

During my adolescent years, several times after my match with Edgar, when I participated in junior competition, and it looked like I was not going to win, Dad would scream from the sidelines, "If you can't play no better than that, then just get off the court." Sometimes he would say, "Your heart is not as big as a mustard seed." Again, Dad was not so much concerned that I was playing as well as I could; his real concern was that I might not win, which for Dad was all-important.

One of Dad's heroes was the legendary football coach Vince Lombardi. According to Dad, Lombardi said, "Winning is not the most important thing—it is the only thing." Vince Lombardi never said this, but Dad's condensed version is not too far off. Among his many sayings, Lombardi said,

> Winning is not a sometime thing: it's an all the time thing. You don't win once in a while; you don't do things right once in a while; you do them right all the time. Winning is a habit. Unfortunately, so is losing. There is no room for second place. There is only one place in my game, and that's first place. I have finished second twice in my time at Green Bay, and I don't ever want to finish second again. There is a second-place Bowl game, but it is a game for losers played by losers. It is and always has been an

American zeal to be first in anything we do, and to win,
and to win, and to win.

It was not until I was an adult that I began to appreciate the circumstances
and forces that had operated on Dad to cause him to think and behave
as he did and to say things to me and my siblings that spurred us to put
forth maximum effort while also causing us to suffer considerable anxiety,
bordering on neurosis, as we endeavored to do so. These circumstances
involved racial oppression as well as difficult personal circumstances
unrelated to race.

From the beginning, the circumstances of Dad's life left him with a
chip on his shoulder. His mother, nee Sadie Edith Boyer, died within a year
of his birth on August 10, 1917, in Chamberlin, Louisiana, in West Baton
Rouge Parish, about ten miles from Baton Rouge. Therefore, the person
who for most of us provides the warmth, comfort, and support in our
infancy, which hopefully leads to our having a healthy sense of well-being,
our mother, was not there to provide these things for him.

One of Sadie's sisters, Edith Ferdinand, who Dad called Aunt Beanie,
stepped up to care for him in her home in Baton Rouge. Aunt Beanie was
married to Britton Ferdinand, and during the time Dad lived with his
aunt and her husband, he was known as Henry Ferdinand. While his
Aunt Beanie and another aunt, Edith, who lived in Port Allen, provided
him warm and comfortable places to live, I suspect they simply did
not—and perhaps could not—provide the nurturing that his mother
would have. Neither did his father or his father's second wife, Rose,
who Dad significantly referred to as Aunt Rose, although he lived long
enough with her for the two to have established the type of relationship
that would have warranted a reference that bespeaks maternal affection
rather than a reference that implies affection but less so than Mom or
Mother.

This is not to say that Dad's early years were not happy. While he
lived primarily with Aunt Beanie, he spent a considerable amount of
time growing up on his maternal grandfather's plantation. Frank
Boyer's plantation was located in Chamberlin, Louisiana, about twelve
miles northwest of Port Allen near the Mississippi River. Frank's father,
Winifred, was Caucasian, and Frank looked Caucasian. I do not know how
Frank came to possess this considerable property, but it would not have
been unusual for a white slave owner like Winifred to have bequeathed
a portion of his property to the family he fathered with his slave lover.
The property was home to Frank and his wife, his son, Henry, who Dad
affectionately referred to as Uncle Son, and Frank's daughters, Dad's

mother, Sadie Edith, and her sisters Mamie, Mildred, Marie Francis and Leola. Mamie was the oldest daughter and was mother to Frank, Edward (known as Booster), Walter, Leola, Mary Francis, and Maude. Mamie was one of the first, if not the first, black women to attend college in Louisiana when she matriculated at Strait College in New Orleans.

A railroad spur connected the plantation to the Mississippi River and was used to transport sugarcane, the farm's main produce, for export. According to Dad, Frank was very disappointed that he did not have more male children who could have worked the plantation. When Dad talked to me about his times on the plantation, he was as animated as I ever saw him. He spoke of the utter joy he experienced when he rode the grounds of the plantation in a horse-drawn buggy and was taken to the Mississippi River where the plantation's sugarcane crop was loaded onto barges. He reckoned that during the peak harvest time, there were as many as two or three hundred men on the plantation cutting the sugar cane with machetes.

Dad's life on the plantation ended abruptly when a dispute arose between Aunt Beanie's husband and Frank, which resulted in his aunt and uncle moving off the plantation and taking Dad with them.

The plantation where Dad spent so much happy time was destroyed by a great flood of the Mississippi river in 1927, a disaster that ironically inspired a song, "Louisiana 1927," by Aaron Neville, the recording star son of a man who was to become Dad's best friend, Phil Neville.

Dad met Phil when Dad's father, having remarried after Dad's mother's death, established a trucking business in New Orleans and brought him to New Orleans to his home at 1102 Valence Street. This residence adjoined the Neville family home. I recently had occasion to speak with Aaron Neville following his performance at Artis Naples, the fine art and performing arts center in Naples, Florida where Al and I live one half the year. He was most engaging and recalled that his father and my father were good friends and that the two families had lived next door to each other. He also told me that my uncle, Reverend Edward Kennedy, had officiated his wedding to his first wife. Dad had a happy childhood in New Orleans where he played sports and became friends with the youngsters in his neighborhood.

Dad's childhood home in New Orleans, Louisiana, at 1102
Valence Street, next door to the Neville family.

Dad's father had two children with Rose: Edward, who became a well-regarded minister and pastored a large and well-known church in New Orleans, and Wilbur, who became a mathematician and systems engineer. Wilbur became an extraordinary and most accomplished person.

After graduating from Southern University, Wilbur worked for several aerospace businesses, including Hughes Aircraft, and was a member of the small team of scientists, engineers, and mathematicians who developed the computer system that guided the first rocket launched into outer space by the United States, an achievement that is commemorated by a plaque bearing his name in the Library of Congress. Wilbur thus provided quantitative expertise to the National Aeronautics and Space Administration years before the black women scientists—Katherine Johnson, Dorothy Vaughn, and Mary Jackson—did so. These women did much to ensure the in-flight safety of *Mercury*, *Gemini*, and *Appollo* astronauts, and the success of John Glenn's historic *Friendship 7* mission in 1962 during which he circled the earth in space orbit. Their amazing story is recounted in the motion picture *Hidden Figures*.

For much of his life, Dad had a cordial but not a close relationship with his two brothers, though he was immensely proud of them, especially of Wilbur. Toward the later years of his life, he reached out to Wilbur, and Wilbur reached back. By the time he died, Dad and Wilbur were quite close

17

and supportive of each other, a support that Wilbur extended in generous measure to my mother for years after Dad died until his own death in 2015. Wilbur would often call to check on her and to offer any assistance she might need.

Another of Dad's relatives who kept in close touch with Mom after his death was Dad's first cousin, Adolphus Kennedy, who before his death in 2019 lived in Daly City, California. More than anyone else on Dad's side of the family, Adolphus sought to maintain contact with us. Not a holiday went by without his calling Mom, Angela, and or myself.

I visited Uncle Wilbur in a nursing home in New Orleans in September 2015 where he was cared for in his final days. Wilbur and his family had evacuated New Orleans because of Hurricane Katrina for Houston, Texas, in August 2005, and he lived there until he requested to return to New Orleans to die after developing a malignant brain tumor. I had come to New Orleans to play the 2015 US Clay Court 65s National Championships. When I walked into Uncle Wilbur's room, it did not appear that he recognized me. His roommate introduced himself to me. On a dresser were several photographs of a man dressed in football uniforms. When I inquired about the photographs, Uncle Wilbur's roommate, who was quite lucid, proudly told me about his professional football career, including the teams and coaches for which he played. The roommate was Roosevelt Grier. He did not mention that after his football career, he provided security services and was a bodyguard for Robert F. Kennedy. He was protecting Ethel Kennedy when Robert Kennedy was assassinated in 1968. He took control of the gun used by the assassin, Sirhan Sirhan, and helped subdue him. I told Grier about Wilbur's accomplishments, and he was very impressed.

Tragically, Dad's other brother was murdered on the streets of New Orleans. Edward was killed by a bomb placed under his car. As far as I know, the murder remains unsolved.

Dad attended Xavier Preparatory School and then Xavier College in New Orleans, but he left after a few months because he could not pay the school's tuition. He then went to live with his mother's sister on Bienville Street and attended Southern University in Baton Rouge. While there, in 1937, he was told by his father that he had inherited seven thousand dollars from his mother at a time when his father's moving and hauling business was not going well, leaving his father almost destitute. Dad gave his father $3,500 in exchange for acquiring half of his father's business. With the other half of the money, he paid fees to attend Dillard University. He completed a total of three and a half years of his studies at the three colleges he attended—Southern, Dillard, and Xavier—but he did not earn a baccalaureate degree from any of them. Rather, during a time when the

NCAA was not vigilant in enforcing its rules regarding compensating student-athletes, Dad spent most of his time playing football. Though small in stature, Dad, who was five foot nine and weighed about 160 pounds, played quarterback at all three schools, whichever one offered him the most financial incentive to do so.

Although he did not receive a college degree, Dad was exposed to several very good professors and serious students, some of whom became his lifelong friends. One of his teammates at Dillard is the father of Shelley Brazier, a very good friend of ours who lives around the corner from our former Washington, DC residence. "Tank" Brazier was a linesman on Dillard's football team when Dad was its quarterback and had blocked for him. Another student Dad knew from Dillard was Shelly's mother. Shelly was thoroughly amused when Dad told her that her mother had been a "stallion," a characterization meaning a stately and beautiful woman, which exemplified the colorful language with which Dad often peppered his conversations, especially with friends.

Another student at Dillard, the most extraordinary of them all, was Mitchell Spellman, who Dad referred to as the "smartest nigger in the world." Mitchell Spellman was indeed one of the smartest people in the world, black or white. Dr. Spellman attended Gilbert Academy in New Orleans, an elite school for young black students seeking college preparatory education, where he was valedictorian of his class. He then attended Dillard where he again was valedictorian of his class. From there, he matriculated at Howard Medical School where he graduated second in his class due to being given a C in a course by the brilliant, but mercurial, Montague Cobb, the first African American to earn a PhD in anthropology, and the only one until after the Korean War.

He trained under Dr. Charles Drew in general surgery at Howard, and from there, he went on to have a brilliant career, the highlights of which included teaching at Howard, Georgetown, Harvard, and UCLA, serving as dean of the Charles Drew Medical School, and founding Harvard Medical International, the mission of which is to develop medical schools around the world in underdeveloped countries. Nelson Mandela said of Dr. Spellman's good works that he alone was responsible for training more than ten thousand physicians.

It is no wonder then that Dad was extremely proud of his association with Dr. Spellman, as am I with his son, Frank Spellman, who is a chip off the old block. Frank has a thriving retinal eye surgery practice and is a wonderful friend, as is his wife Beverly.

At Dr. Spellman's funeral held at the chapel of Georgetown Preparatory School in Maryland where Frank had attended, Al, after listening to speaker after speaker talk about Dr. Spelman's accomplishments, leaned over and whispered in my ear, "Dad was right. He was the smartest nigger in the world."

Dad was one of the most informed persons I have ever known. He voraciously read newspapers and articles, especially those published by black media. He was a devoted reader of *Ebony, The Washington Post, Jet,* the *Washington Informer,* and the *Afro American.* He was deeply suspicious of the press, however, a suspicion he frequently expressed by saying, "Paper don't care what's written on it."

Some of the most constructive and instructive times in my life were when Dad, my younger brother, Randy, and I would get into discussions and debates about public policy or race issues at the dinner table. One could not be a shrinking violet during those animated conversations. Also, it was not a time when you could afford to get your feelings hurt or let on that you were offended. Without regard to a person's feelings, if any one of us felt that the position another took was not well thought out or had not been sufficiently discerning of what the truth was despite press bias, we would say so in no uncertain terms and would express wonderment that the holder of the position could be so gullible.

I cannot recall ever hearing the word *nigger* spoken before Dad used it. He simply loved the word and employed it frequently when describing any perceived attribute possessed by an African American. Thus, he would say, "He is the dumbest nigger I know," "He is one bad nigger," "He is nigger rich," or "That nigger's so poor he squeaks when he walks."

Dad's penchant for using the N-word led Al to take him aside shortly before our daughter Morgan was born to earnestly ask him to refrain from using it in the presence of the child we were expecting. She explained that children are like parrots. They simply repeat what they hear without knowing the meaning of their words or calibrating the appropriateness of what they say.

To Dad's credit, he refrained from using the word in our children's presence. While Dad refrained from using the N-word, he still used other colorful terms to refer to African Americans, including *boot, coon, spook, splib,* and, his second-favorite reference, *skiboo.*

It is ironic that the slur nigger was both the title and subject of my brother's most controversial and best- selling book, *Nigger: The Strange Career of a Troublesome Word.* My brother Randall is a Harvard Law School professor. When Randy told me that he had been invited to give the prestigious Tanner Lecture at Stanford University and that he could talk about anything he chose and that he had chosen to talk about the word *nigger,* I argued vehemently with him about the wisdom of writing about this most despised word. I am glad that I was not successful and am so proud of my brother's willingness over the years to comment on the most controversial of subjects with honesty and intelligence.

Many times cited for his intellectual insight as a public intellectual, Randy has received well-deserved honors, including honorary degrees from Bard College, Occidental College, and Haverford College, and the Robert Kennedy award for his book *Race, Crime, and the Law.*

After attending college, Dad enlisted in the army on March 12, 1941, following a major disagreement with his father.

Dad neither forgot nor forgave the indignities to which he was subjected by whites, particularly by those in authority. I saw this firsthand and the effect on this very proud man. When we would drive to South Carolina from DC in the summer to visit relatives, we sometimes would be stopped by white state troopers or local police. Invariably, they would call Dad by his first or middle name with obvious delight in front of his wife and children, although the officers had been given Dad's license, which quite clearly bore his first, middle, and last names. Thus, for example, they would say, "Harold, you were going a little too fast, do you know that?" Note that this required him to respond to the obvious effort at humiliation, thereby intensifying that effort. For miles thereafter, Dad, normally a very loquacious man, was silent.

Dad's inclination to neither forget nor forgive the indignities he suffered stuck with him throughout his life. His racial views were cemented and affected every view he had regarding anything in which race was an issue. He was a race man to the core, and the attitude that this designation signifies infused his every reaction to any matter in which race might come into play. For example, one did not have to ask him for whom he was rooting in any athletic contest, events of enormous importance and significance to Dad, as they were to many blacks. Simply put, whichever team had the most black players or had a black coach or black quarterback was the team Dad backed. It is Dad's life experiences that more than anything else caused Dad to insist that Randy, Angela, and I prepare ourselves to be people who no one would disrespect on account of race or otherwise without a significant consequence.

The circumstances of Dad's life had a profound influence on his outlook on other things as well. Dad's maternal family lost their land due to flooding and, for that reason, came upon hard financial times. His father always struggled financially and had to borrow money from him to keep his business afloat. With respect to money, then, Dad taught it was vitally important that one be frugal, self-sufficient, and dutiful in financially caring for his family. This is why he insisted on our family living on his salary, leaving Mom's more substantial salary to be devoted to savings.

Dad's view of a man's obligation to his family led him, as it does me, to be condemning of men, particularly black men, who are not dutiful to their families. Any man worthy of being called a man does all he can to support and defend his family. He certainly does not embarrass the family or do things that result in its destruction as I have witnessed all too often. I know black men who are very educated and have professional titles who have done both despite having fathers who have shown them the way by loving and supporting their wives and families for years and under the most trying of circumstances.

These men without shame abdicate their responsibilities. Among other transgressions, they not only have adulterous affairs but are extraordinarily inept when it comes to concealing their conduct. Who takes a mistress to the same restaurant he has frequented with his wife and family on family outings? One would think that these men—all privileged and the products of intact families themselves—would appreciate that black families have been an indispensable ingredient to the survival of blacks in this country. Even when we could not legally marry, black men and women committed themselves to each other and raised families that endured and overcame all manner of oppression and indignities. These men who wallow in denial regarding the shamefulness of their conduct, in violating moral principles and the vows made to their wives, also dishonor the many black men who have advanced the cause over the years by building and maintaining families. These men must surely know that their offspring, especially their daughters, will find it very difficult to trust their hearts to another and establish the kind of relationship that would be the basis for establishing the next generation of families.

To this point, one of the scenes in my favorite movie, *The Godfather*, resonates greatly with me. Johnny Fontaine, an actor and singer living in Los Angeles, returns to New York City to attend the Godfather's daughter's wedding to a celebrity welcome. When Fontaine and the Godfather are alone, Fontaine whimpers to the Godfather about not being offered a part in a movie by a big-shot producer that would revive his declining career. The Godfather grabs Fontaine by the arm, mocks his complaining, and then slaps him while asking him whether he was taking care of his family. If Fontaine had said anything other than that he was caring for his family the Godfather would not have helped him to get the part he so desperately desired. He certainly would not have made the producer an "offer he could not refuse." I still recoil at the iconic scene showing the severed bloody head of the producer's prized Arabian thoroughbred, Khartoum, in the producer's bed beside the producer as he slept. Fontaine was given the part.

Dad presumed that white people were racist, and he treated them accordingly until they showed otherwise. In assessing blacks, particularly black leaders, Dad was of the view that if white people liked a black person, that was reason enough to be suspicious of that person insofar as his being a race man was concerned. Likewise, if a black person was disliked, even despised by whites, then Dad generally liked that person for that reason alone. Nothing showed this better than Dad's embrace of Idi Amin, the president of Uganda from 1971 to 1979. No matter how vigorously Randy and I would denounce Amin armed with all manner of information regarding Amin's atrocities, Dad embraced him.

Dad loved it that Amin took on the title "His Excellency President for Life, Field Marshal Alhaji Dr. Idi Amin Dada, VC, DSO, MC, CBE (Conqueror of the British Empire)." As long as he was feared by whites, Dad was willing to overlook Amin's human rights abuses, political repression, ethnic persecutions, extrajudicial killings, nepotism, corruption, and gross economic mismanagement. It occurs to me that Donald Trump's supporters have a similar allegiance to this man. Consequently, no matter how crude, seemingly unfit, or morally corrupt, they support him—even love him—because he shakes things up and, I believe, appears to put blacks and women in what they believe is their rightful subservient positions.

Dad's presumption that a white person was racist could be overcome. And, it was, sometimes by the most unlikely of people. One such person was William "Bill" Riordan. Riordan was a freewheeling tennis agent and promoter who managed the early careers of Jimmy Connors, Illie Nastasie, and Cliff Richey and promoted a series of lucrative but falsely labeled "winner-take-all" televised tennis matches featuring Connors.

Dad met Bill Riordan through Randy, who had become a very good tennis player by the time he was sixteen. Randy played a tournament in Salisbury, Maryland, where Riordan lived and was the tournament director. Randy and Riordan's son, Billy, were doubles partners. One evening Randy, who was staying in the Riordan's home, overheard Riordan refer to "niggers."

Randy told Dad about what Riordan had said. One naturally would think that Dad would have had a very negative reaction, but he did not. Rather, circumstances conspired and Dad and Bill Riordan, a member of the John Birch Society, became very good friends. They were very much alike, both were strongly opinionated and very much admired the art of the hustle. They liked to frequent horse racing tracks and gamble. They daringly exhibited their eccentricities and got much pleasure from pulling one over on the uptight members of any organization—the stuffier, the better.

When Dad, Randy, and I went to England to attend Wimbledon in 1978, the second year of Randy's studies as a Rhodes Scholar at Oxford, we were allowed to enter the VIP tent on the grounds of the tournament on Riordan's say so. Riordan, the agent for Jimmy Connors who was the number one seed in the tournament, was a frequent VIP visitor and a person tournament officials would not want to cross. Riordan introduced us as African royalty from Nigeria, Dad as Chief Arumba, whose land had an oil field on it, and his two sons, Randy as Prince Wasuku and me as Prince Mantubu.

We were treated deferentially and catered to like I had never experienced, before or since. It was during this trip that Riordan's nephew, the grandson of John Paul Getty, who was accompanying Riordan, took such a liking to Randy, Dad, and me that he chose to stay with us at the very modest bed-and-breakfast where we were staying while attending Wimbledon rather than with Riordan who was staying at the five-star hotel where the top players were staying.

It was also during this trip that Riordan took us to the Playboy Club in London where he gave Randy and me a hundred dollars each with which to gamble. We lost all the money but had a grand time watching many of the players who were participating in the tournament squire around gorgeous women.

Dad and Mr. Riordan were loyal to their friends to a fault, and they trusted each other so much that I also came to trust Mr. Riordan. I asked him for his advice and to invest money I had accumulated when I was in high school. A couple of years later, Riordan presented me with a check for twice the amount I had given him. I am sure that this was not because of Riordan's investment know-how but from his generosity for the son of a friend.

Dad retired in 1973, when he was fifty-five years old, after thirty years of government service, twenty-six years and five months at the post office, and four years and seven months in the military. He then worked for the DC Department of Recreation where he ran tennis programs at playgrounds and recreation centers throughout the city, including the recreation centers in some of the most hardscrabble neighborhoods in the city, including Kenilworth, King Greenleaf, Congress Heights, and Langley. Dad's tennis programs afforded him the opportunity to interact with numerous youngsters, teaching them tennis and life lessons, something he enjoyed immensely. This work inspired the words on a plaque installed at the Takoma tennis courts in the neighborhood where my family lived that were dedicated in his honor and to his memory shortly after he died. The plaque reads, "Mr. Kennedy inspired many Washingtonians, especially youngsters, to play tennis to the best of their abilities. These courts were his school."

Plague at the public courts at Third and Van Buren Street across the street from the Takoma Recreation Center.

Dad died in the Veterans Administration Hospital in Washington, DC, on September 16, 2002, the day before we were to bring him home to die there as he wished. He was eighty-four years old. Despite their valiant efforts, the VA doctors could not determine the source of the sepsis that was ravaging his body following the amputation of part of his foot. That I was not able to get him home where he would take his last breath is one of my significant regrets.

3 CHAPTER
MY MOTHER

According to one of her birth certificates, my mother, nee Rachel Thelma Spann, was born on February 16, 1924. Another birth certificate, also containing the seal of the state of South Carolina and other indicia of authenticity, indicates she was born February 12, 1924, in Great Falls, S.C. Mom attempted to conceal her birth place her entire life as she did not like being born in a "back-water" place like Great Falls. We celebrated her birthday on February 12.

My mother

Mom's parents were Lillian White Spann and Sellars Spann. Lillian, the matriarch of our family until her death and who our family affectionately called Big Mama, was born December 29, 1888, just twenty-three years after the end of slavery, in Sumter, South Carolina, to Osborne and Rachel

White, both of whom died when she was very young: Osborne at fifty-three years old in December 1907 and Rachel at thirty-six in June 1900. This means that there is a high probability that my great-grandparents were born into slavery. It is also probable that my great-grandmother, as were countless black women, was raped by her white overseer or master, though the law did not recognize this perfidy as such, which accounts for my grandmother's light complexion.

After the death of her birth parents, Big Mama lived with her grandparents, the Robinsons, and then was "adopted" by the Rhames family. Adopted is in quotes because I do not know, but I doubt that she was legally and formally adopted in accordance with South Carolina law. It is much more likely that she was taken in by the Rhames family out of compassion because the need was there.

Big Mama married Marcellus "Sellars" Spann of Batesburg, South Carolina, in a ceremony in the Rhames family's home. Sellars, born about 1860, the same year Abraham Lincoln was selected as the US presidential candidate for the Republican Party and the state of South Carolina became the first state to secede from the union, was the son of Paul and Anna Watson Spann. Sellars had several brothers and sisters, Arthur, Julius, Paul, and half sisters and brothers born to Paul's second wife, Beatrice Mamie Coleman, George, Clara, John, Beatrice, Ruby, and Mamie. Sellars worked as a chauffeur.

Big Mama and Sellars had five children, Anna, Sylvester, LeRoy ("Bubba"), Lillian, and my mother. Theirs was not a happy marriage. Sellars drank heavily and abused his wife and their children. Mom confided to my wife that she did not have one good memory of her father. One terrible memory of him was when she and her mother returned from the funeral of Sellars brother, Julius, which Sellars had not attended. Mom and her mother saw policemen in the yard of their home on McDuffie Street in Columbia. They were investigating his death. Sellars had been found dead in the street.

Big Mama was a churchgoing woman, a devoted member of Wesley United Methodist Church, located on Gervais Street in Columbia, which she attended every Sunday along with her children. She maintained a sense of dignity at all times and instructed all of her children about the importance of cleanliness and "good manners," the latter trait being more important than almost any other, including intelligence. The imperative of having good manners was taught to Mom and was passed down to Angela, Randy, and me as was the importance of education. Looking back, it is clear that the instruction regarding the importance of good manners was intended to and did convey much more than a knowledge and appreciation for etiquette. Rather, it was a way of insisting upon behavior that would help in keeping us safe and convey to the observer that we were a product of good breeding, thus making us more desirable as employees and mates in marriage.

Big Mama was an early riser; each morning at sunrise, she would sweep the dirt in front of the porch of her big rambling white-frame house at 1010 Oak Street in Columbia. The dirt was left with a neat appearance that showed the brushstrokes of Big Mama's broom.

Big Mama's ownership of her home was remarkable given that she was black and female, two characteristics making it very likely that she purchased her home for cash, money saved from her income from cleaning homes and working as a seamstress. It is very unlikely that any financial institution in the segregated South would have provide her a mortgage.

Mom attended segregated Booker T. Washington High School in Columbia, and she was a very good student. She embraced her mother's guidance to get an education because "they can't take that away from you." Mom readily accepted this advice, desiring a better life for herself and her family than could be provided by cleaning other people's homes, as she had learned to do when helping her mother who earned income for such work or as a seamstress, another source of income, when her mother worked for Haltiwangers, a department store in Columbia. Mom passed along the instruction most forcefully to Angela, Randy, and me.

Big Mama cautioned her daughters about not being too "fast" and remaining chaste. They certainly were not to go to the USO at the corner of Gervais and Oak Street, which was within walking distance of their home. The USO was where the soldiers stationed at Fort Jackson socialized, and everyone knew what the soldiers were interested in.

Mom, at the time sixteen years old, having just graduated from high school, always independent and adventuresome even at this young age, violated her mother's injunction and, along with Naomi Lewis, a beautiful neighborhood friend whose sister had been selected as Miss Sepia, the black Miss America, went to the USO.

There she met Dad, who was stationed at Fort Jackson. There was an immediate attraction between them. Dad was an exceedingly handsome twenty-four-year-old soldier in uniform. Mom was equally attractive despite having had one of her breasts removed, for reasons of which I am unaware, when she was thirteen or fourteen years old and left with disfiguring scars.

Mom and Naomi Lewis

They were married four months later on November 21, 1942, by a justice of the peace in Lexington, South Carolina, a suburb of Columbia, for which they were charged three dollars. Dad tipped the officiant two dollars. Mom loved to tell about how handsome Dad was in his uniform and how he taught her to French kiss.

One of the things about Mom that attracted Dad was her remarkable joie de vivre, a characteristic Mom demonstrated her entire life, including after Dad's death. When she was just a few months shy of her ninety-second birthday, she—accompanied by her live-in boyfriend, Paul Williams—took a cruise off the coast of South America although she had suffered three strokes within the preceding twelve months. On this trip, she suffered her fourth stroke, the complications from which ended her life. I am comforted in knowing that she would not have wanted it any other way.

I also am comforted in knowing that after Dad's death, Mom had the exceedingly good fortune of meeting Williams, a widower and an intelligent and caring man who was interested in and knowledgeable about many things, including his passion: brain mapping. For thirteen years, he and Mom lived together, traveled, and attended lectures and presentations by well-known speakers. They also visited the White House several times for social engagements with Michelle and Barack Obama.

Mom with her friends Bettie Currie, President Clinton's secretary, and Marion Robinson, Michelle Obama's mother, at a party at the White House.

Mom knew Michelle Obama through Angela who was Michelle's Princeton roommate. During short school year breaks, such as during Thanksgiving, Michelle would often stay with Mom and Dad, rather than incur the expense of traveling to her hometown, Chicago. Michelle was a bridesmaid in Angela's wedding, and they remain good friends.

Once while at the White House to attend a party, Mom drank too much and was taken by Michelle to her and the president's bed to recover Mom loved to tell the story of how she had been in President Obama's bed.

Shortly after Mom's death, when I called Paul to offer my condolences, he said, "You know, Henry, some people never have the kind of relationship Rachel and I had." I was moved to tears and was very grateful that my mother had been loved and cared for by two men who would have done anything for her.

Mom attended South Carolina State College, a historically black college, in Orangeburg, South Carolina, after graduating from Booker T. Washington High School, where she graduated in 1942. Mom was a very good student and engaged in many extracurricular activities, including the school's YWCA chapter of which she was president, the choir and drama clubs, and the Delta Sigma Theta sorority.

One of Mom's fellow students at South Carolina State was Essie Mae Washington, the daughter of Senator Strom Thurmond and Carrie Butler, an African American domestic servant for Thurmond's parents. Mom saw Thurmond several times when he came to South Carolina State to visit his daughter. Thurmond would drive up in his large black Cadillac and meet his daughter at the home of the president of the college. When the press many years later reported that Thurmond had fathered a black child—information that was shocking and new to most white Americans—it was old news to many black Americans.

Because South Carolina State did not admit married students, Mom deceived school authorities regarding her marital status. Dad, in the meantime, was performing military service. He sent his monthly salary allotments to Mom, which she dutifully kept without spending any of them.

Once when Dad came to visit Mom when she was still in college, he hailed a taxi to take them to a hotel in Columbia. The taxi driver recognized Mom and not knowing that she was married to Dad, angrily told him that he would not drive Mrs. Spann's daughter to a hotel where should be taken advantage of. Instead, he would take her to 1010 Oak Street where he knew her mother lived and would tell her mother that she was being victimized by an older man, a soldier. Afraid that Mom's mother would find out that he and Mom were married from a taxi driver, Dad quickly went to Big Mama's house to tell her himself. When he arrived at the house, Big Mama was on the front porch. He began to tell her of his marriage to Mom, but in the middle of his explanation, the five-foot-nine, 150-pound former college quarterback faced with the four-foot-ten seamstress weighing no more than 100 pounds suddenly fainted.

Big Mama forgave Dad for his deception and rather quickly came to like and trust him. For his part, Dad returned her affection and, despite her diminutive size, fondly referred to her as Big Lil and did everything he could to be a good son-in-law.

Upon graduation from South Carolina State, Mom and Dad lived at 1010 Oak Street with Big Mama. Dad became the enforcer of the rules Big Mama had for the men who rented the rooms that were under her house. Among these rules, and by far the most important, after the timely payment of rent, was that no roomer could have a woman in his room at any time. If a roomer violated the rule, Dad would remind him that Big Mama demanded strict compliance with the rule and that another infraction would result in eviction, which at this time of laissez-faire landlord tenant relations meant that a lock would be put on the door, thereby preventing the roomer from reentering. Dad also was the collector of the rent—all in cash of course. Late payment was not tolerated, and Dad so informed each of the roomers.

After graduating from South Carolina State, Mom attended New York University to obtain her master of arts degree in elementary education, which was conferred on her on October 27, 1952. She attended New York University at the state of South Carolina's expense because the state would not permit her to attend the University of South Carolina or any other school it funded that offered such a degree because she was black.

One large impediment to Mom attending graduate school outside of South Carolina was that she had a two-year-old, me, who needed to be cared for. She did not have to look far to find someone she could trust to take care of me. Her older sister, Lillian Bell, readily volunteered. Although I have no memory of this time, I can extrapolate from what was told to me years later that my Aunt Lillian cared for me with loving kindness and treated me as if I were her own son. It is for that reason that her children, my first cousins, Thaddeus, Gary, Veta, and Reginald, are like brothers and a sister to me. I have been told that when Mom came to retrieve me from Aunt Lillian's home after completing her studies at NYU, I cried upon learning that I would have to go with her, exclaiming, "You are not my mother."

Aunt Lillian, for many years a dedicated special education teacher in rural communities near Columbia, was the sweetest woman I have ever known, generous to a fault and possessed of a remarkable capacity to grieve. Aunt Lillian would attend the funerals of persons she hardly knew just so she could pay her respects and grieve with their family members. Her ability to grieve was in full display at Dad's funeral where the crescendo of her wails easily exceeded the sobs of all others.

While sweet, Aunt Lillian was not reluctant to express her dissatisfaction in strong and pointed terms about what she considered to be undesirable conduct. When such behavior was done by blacks she would often say, "Niggers make my ass hurt." When done by whites, she just as often would say, "Crackers make my ass hurt."

Mom never forgot the generosity of her sister, and they remained very close. Mom remained very close to her other sister, Anna Price, as well. The sisters would talk almost every morning beginning at five thirty. The warmth and closeness of which they were proud and valued to the utmost was passed on to their children and explain the closeness of the "Spann clan," my first cousins, which continues to this day, grows stronger with every passing year, and is enlivened by well-attended biennial reunions.

Mom became a master teacher, teaching third and fourth grade at Waverly Elementary School in Columbia. When we moved to Washington, after teaching in the DC public schools for two years, she taught at Chevy

Chase Elementary School, which is located in an upscale suburb adjacent to the District of Columbia in Montgomery County, Maryland.

Teaching at Chevy Chase was very important to Mom. For many years, she was the only black teacher there.

For many years her white colleagues were cruelly dismissive of her. She spoke with pain about being snubbed. Early on, fellow teachers would engage in conversations in which she was ostentatiously excluded. While others would be invited to dinners or parties or various sorts of get-togethers, she would receive no such invitations. Parents, without cause, complained about her teaching their children. Their assumption was that, because she was black, she could not possibly be as good as her white counterparts.

From the outset, though, there were a few colleagues who were supportive. Mom always spoke highly of her principal, Mr. Powers. In her view, he treated her fairly and respectfully. Mom always spoke about two fellow teachers with tremendous fondness as well. One was Dee Seegers, and the other was Esther Pizer. Mom became genuinely close to them.

Over time, mom became less isolated at Chevy Chase. For one thing, she developed a reputation as a no-nonsense disciplinarian with a gift for teaching reading and writing. Parents began to request that she be their children's teacher. She was deeply pleased by that development.

As it turns out, Mom taught many of the sons and daughters of the professional elite of Washington and its suburbs, including the children of Patricia Wald and David Tatel, esteemed judges on the United States court of appeals for the District of Columbia Circuit, and Marna Tucker and Lawrence Baskir, respectively a well-regarded lawyer and judge on the Court of Federal Claims.

Her colleagues also increasingly warmed to her. The ones who had been hostile tended to be the older teachers. They retired or died off. Younger teachers were drawn to Mom, as she was always young at heart.

Chevy Chase changed mom's racial views. The overt, unapologetic white racism that was pervasive in South Carolina scarred my Mother. For a long time, her presumption was that virtually all white people looked down upon her as they did all black people. She was afraid of white people and distrusted them. Somehow, though, her negative feelings toward white adults did not infect her relationships with white children. She loved her students—all of them—even in the early years at Chevy Chase when she felt alone and constantly exposed to a hostile gaze that awaited her failure.

Mom's third grade class at Chevy Chase Elementary School

As time passed, however, the broadly negative view that she had about whites gave way to a more nuanced view. As she became friendly with more whites, she became more willing to make distinctions based on personal attributes. She was asked to teach a course for teachers in Montgomery County on how to handle race issues at their schools, an assignment she tackled with enthusiasm and pride.

When Mom retired, Chevy Chase held an all-school gathering to mark the occasion. She was deeply touched. The Montgomery County public school bureaucracy movingly brought home to all assembled the high esteem that Mother had earned through her many years of devoted service. Part of the celebration included the planting of a tree in front of the school in her honor. In the end, Mom was extremely proud of her association with the Chevy Chase Elementary School.

My relationship with Mom was complicated and changed over the years. I always loved her dearly and was immensely impressed and proud of her intelligence, courage, willingness, and capacity to stand up to racism and sexism, and her remarkable joie de vivre. Further, she was singularly ambitious while suffering low-grade depression for most of her life, a condition she managed with unusual fortitude.

These strong points eclipsed her less-than-admirable traits. Primary among these were her self-centeredness and vanity. Her vanity was in full display when Mom, in order to wear fashionable pointed-toe stiletto heels, had the bones in her pinkie toes surgically removed.

Mom, the youngest of her siblings, rejoiced in and was prideful of her youthful appearance and spirit. It was a standing joke in our family that when Mom was asked her age, depending upon the circumstances, she would either decline to answer at all or, more often, lie, saying her age was at least ten or fifteen years younger than it was.

Mom's deceptions regarding her age were mostly amusing. One such time was when Mom received an award for her work heading a program that instructed Montgomery County teachers and school administrators on how to handle racial and diversity issues. Mom asked me to prepare her résumé for the group giving her the award. When I asked Mom about the dates of her graduation from college and graduate school and other dates that typically appear on a résumé, she refused to disclose this information, saying, "They don't need to know all that, and if they do, they can keep their award."

While this was a time when Mom's vanity was mostly and simply amusing, at other times, her vanity made me furious. One time was when we should have been consoling each other over Dad's death. We had just visited Stewart's funeral home to view Dad's body and were preparing for his memorial service when I received a call from the writer of the notice and obituary that was to appear in the *Washington Post*. He wanted to know how long Mom and Dad had been married. When I asked Mom to provide this information, she refused because to reveal the length of their marriage would permit the extrapolation of her approximate age. This was particularly infuriating to me because more than anything else of which Dad was proud was his marriage to Mom. Dad would want it shouted from the hilltop that he and Mom had been married a very long time. That Mom knew this but nevertheless would not disclose it reflected that even at this moment—the time of Dad's death—for Mom, it was all about her.

This was particularly roiling given my efforts to bring Dad home to live out his final days. To that end, it was necessary to have a bed put on the first floor of their home because Dad could not take the stairs to their bedroom. Mom would not allow a bed to be put on the first floor because it would not be aesthetically pleasing.

After several years of resentment, my displeasure waned, and there was an instauration of the respect I had for her as I came to admire her herculean efforts to live a full life while she faced increasing serious health issues that accompanied her advancing years.

4 CHAPTER

EARLY YEARS IN COLUMBIA, SOUTH CAROLINA

After being honorably discharged from the army in October 1945, from Camp Livingston, Louisiana, Dad found a job as a laborer in Columbia, South Carolina, as a mover for the American Express Company, a business that moved merchandise by railroad. After working for American Express for about a month, Dad ran into Clifford "Speedy" Johnson, from Louisiana, whom he had met during his time in the army. Together they bought and operated the Moonlight Grill—according to Dad, the "hottest nightclub in town." To advertise the establishment's opening they had five hundred flyers made and put them in the mailboxes of residents who lived near the fairgrounds in Columbia near where the Moonlight Grill was located.

The nightclub lasted for about a year and a half, but it was forced to close when it was raided by state law enforcement authorities. Dad was thrown in jail for selling liquor without a license. Upon the advice of an older cellmate, he called a lawyer named Prince who bailed him out of jail for $50. Dad went to court, got in line with others who were charged with similar offenses, and was sentenced to a fine of $75.

Thereafter, Dad and Speedy sold the Moonlight Grill to Sam Taylor for $300, which they split evenly between them. Following the sale of the Moonlight Grill, Dad got a job as a custodian at the Veterans Administration at Fort Jackson. "Talking about a good job, I should still be there ... I knew the major." Dad had a small office that was outfitted with a small coffee maker. He got to know the white officers who asked him to do small side jobs for them and gave him generous tips.

After leaving the army, Dad became a United States postal clerk.

He and Raymond Weston became the first blacks to secure mail carrier positions in South Carolina in forty years. Dad did not last in this position long. "Everything I did was wrong. I picked up so many demerits it wasn't funny." He was allowed to resign after about seven months.

Dad then went to Allen University, a historically black college in Columbia, which was founded in 1870 by a number of ministers of the African Methodist Episcopal Church, including John M. Brown, a bishop in the African American Episcopal Church and a leader in the underground railroad. Allen's Chappelle Auditorium was the site of the meeting of educators and lawyers to initiate efforts that led to the landmark US Supreme Court case *Brown v. Board of Education* (1954) on school integration. Dad went to Allen on the GI Bill "for the money," $90 per month.

After matriculating at Allen for four months, Dad took the Railway Mail Carrier examination, passed, and started work in 1949 sorting mail on trains that traveled to cities up and down the East Coast.

After working as a railway mail carrier, Dad carried mail in South Carolina, delivering it by truck in small towns not far from Columbia. Several times, he was harassed by the Ku Klux Klan and told more than once that he could not perform his job in the towns where the Klan held power. He was told that he would be killed if he continued to come to those towns.

I was born February 22, 1948, six years after my parents were married.

One of my first childhood memories is of trying to build a swimming pool in the backyard of the home my parents built at 1555 Farm View Street. I was about six years old when I decided that I would dig a large hole in the backyard in which to install a pool that I envisioned would be my personal swimming place where I could swim to my heart's content and not have to wait for someone to take me to the Drew pool, the large segregated public pool named for the great black physician Charles Drew. I learned how to swim there, and it was one of the few places where blacks could go for recreation. Day after day, I would shovel in the spot I had selected for my pool, but, for some reason, inexplicable to me at the time, when I would finally manage to shovel enough dirt to create a hole of some depth, the opening would suddenly fill back up. I never figured out that Dad would throw dirt back in the hole in the evening when I was asleep when it started to get deep. All summer, I kept digging that hole without ever making any headway.

Me at six years old.

This penchant to continue an effort even when doing so clearly does not advance my aim was confirmed as one of my psychological traits many years later when I submitted to psychological testing in conjunction with my treatment for depression. That testing, and prior testing at Princeton as part of a researcher's project, show that I am abnormally inflexible and not one to readily discern the futility of trying to put a square peg in a round hole long after most people would have determined that something different should be tried. This trait, while at times quite problematic, also has served me well. A feature of that inflexibility is perseverance, a quality that is important to have in order to accomplish goals that others see as unrealistic.

The home Mom and Dad built on Farm View
Street in Columbia, South Carolina.

The home built by Mom and Dad was on land they purchased chiefly using the military allotment money Dad had sent Mom when he was on active duty in the military. They purchased several lots of land, all of which they sold except for the one on which they built their attractive ranch-style house. A prominent feature of the house was a very large fireplace in the living room surrounded by a cushioned seating area. A bountiful fig tree graced the front yard of our house, which was across a road from a large field where cows grazed.

My most vividly remembered experience during this time was when I was six years old and I went to the small grocery store that was close to our house to get my favorite snack: a large dill pickle wrapped in a white paper napkin. When it came time to pay for the pickle, I apparently touched the hand of the young white woman cashier while she was giving me change, thereby violating the convention in South Carolina at the time. A black customer when he was due change would collect it only after it was placed on the counter and would not take it directly from the hand of a white cashier to avoid human contact.

I took my change directly from the cashier's hand. Upon seeing this, a white man, a very big one, cursed and chased me out of the store and yelled at me not to ever come back. I was terrified and did not know what I had done to warrant this man's fury.

I ran home and told Mom about what happened. Dad was delivering mail. When he returned home, Mom told him of my incident at the store. Dad became enraged. He went to their bedroom and got a pistol, and in front of us, inserted bullets in the gun's chambers. When he headed for the door, my mother grabbed him around his legs and hugged them tightly screaming "Ken No!" over and over again, restraining him from going to confront the couple at the store.

Much later, I realized that my father's rage over my mistreatment likely would have had tragic consequences but for my mother's determined intervention. As Dad told Randy many years later, if he had stayed in Columbia, he either would have killed someone or he would have been killed.

Perhaps, going through my father's mind when he grabbed his gun was what had happened to another black youngster, Emmett Till, at about the same time as my encounter at the grocery store. Fourteen-year-old Emmet Till was beaten, shot dead, and then mutilated in Money, Mississippi, because he had allegedly spoken to a white woman, Carolyn Bryant, in a suggestive way—an allegation that the woman recanted in 2016. Coincidentally, Till's nickname was Bobo, mine was Boobie. Like me, Till, who had gone to the Bryant's store to buy candy, stuttered, which perhaps accounted for what some onlookers perceived as a "wolf whistle" directed at Carolyn. Press reports of this tragic event states that Till's mother said that Till had particular difficulty pronouncing *b* sounds, and he may have whistled to overcome problems asking for bubble gum.

Randy's godmother, Eloise Randolph, lived directly across the street from Big Mama, and her husband took me to the Columbia Township Auditorium to see what undoubtedly was one of the best live pop performances of all times. On the same stage and performing back to back were Bill Haley and the Comets, singing "Rock around the Clock," Little Anthony and the Imperials, singing "I'm on the Outside Looking In" and "Tears on My Pillow," Danny and the Juniors, singing "At the Hop," and Frankie Lyman and the Teenagers, singing "Why Do Fools Fall in Love?" To this day, I have not enjoyed a live musical performance as much.

My godmother, Eva DeVault, also provided wonderful experiences.

One of a kind! My godmother, Eva DeVault cutting up, perhaps doing a jig that was a precursor to twerking. Mylie Cyrus has nothing on my godmother!

Eva was one of a kind. She and Mom had become friends when they both were students at South Carolina State. Eva was dark skinned, short, smart, extremely witty, and the only person I have ever known who was able to outtalk both my mother and father—combined! An elementary school teacher, Eva was a natural-born performer who, at a different time, would have been a superb professional standup comedian in the vein of

Moms Mabley. When Eva walked into the room, everyone shut down and watched her work. She frequently used her husband, my godfather, David "Bubsie" DeVault, as an unwitting prop and straight man. Bubsie was as quiet as Eva was lively and ebullient.

In family settings, Eva knew she was expected to entertain—and she did, never failing to deliver, often bringing her props with her. When we would visit her home on Greenview Street on the outskirts of Columbia, a home with a backyard surrounded by a fence with a large sign that announced "Keep Out, Bad Dog," she would invariably find a reason to show all in attendance her proficiency in playing the conga drums, bongos, or tambourine or how to approach the line in a bowling alley to execute a proper release of a bowling ball, all the while showing off her new bowling shoes and bowling outfits. Interspersed in these demonstrations were hilarious, perfectly timed ribald one-liners complete with Eva describing what Bubsie was really thinking as he saw her perform.

When Eva died, nobody was surprised that Bubsie also died within a year, officially of an unknown cause but to those who knew Eva and Bubsie, it is clear that he simply did not want to go on living without her.

Shortly before he died, one of Bubsie's sisters summoned me to his hospital bed. Feeble and dying, he presented me with a sword carried by a union officer in the Civil War. It now is displayed in my Alexandria home. For me, it symbolizes the struggles of my ancestors, particularly the black men who taught by example and courageously endured life's slings and arrows to ultimately prevail.

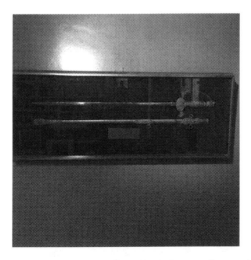

The sword carried by a Union officer during the Civil Ward bequeathed to me by my godfather, David DeVault.

41

Not long after I was threatened and run out of the deli, Dad had yet another encounter with the Ku Klux Klan. My parents sold their Farm View Street home and moved to Washington, DC. In doing so, they became a part of the great migration in the 1950s and 1960s of black families out of the South to the North to escape oppression and the lack of opportunity they were experiencing on a day-to-day basis in the states of their births.

5 CHAPTER
MOVE TO WASHINGTON, DC

The house in which we lived in Columbia was quite commodious. By contrast, the two-bedroom apartment at the Parklands apartment complex in southeast Washington where we first lived in DC was anything but. There was nothing parklike about it. It was cramped and was located in a very modest neighborhood in the poorest area of the city. The apartment had a combined living and dining area and two bedrooms, one containing a bunk bed where Randy and I slept and the other where my parents slept.

We moved from Parklands after a year into a townhouse that was just a shade larger than our apartment in Parklands but was in a solidly black middle-class neighborhood in Northwest DC. We lived at 730 Tewksbury Place for only a year before moving four blocks away to 6600 Seventh Street, NW, the house where I grew up and would be the family home until both my parents died.

The home in which I grew up at 6600 Seventh Street, NW

Our home at 6600 Seventh Street NW was chosen by Dad primarily because he thought it was ideally located. It was just three blocks from a recreation center that offered every kind of sports facility to provide boys a place to pursue athletic endeavors. This location, however, was not the choice of Mom who much preferred to live on Washington's "Gold" Coast or in the "Flowers," so named for the streets of the neighborhood taken from the names of flowers and plants west of Sixteenth Street in upper Northwest Washington where Washington's black professional class lived or, as mother would say, where the "can't she, don't she" reside.

Almost every Sunday, when returning home from church services at Asbury United Methodist Church, Mom insisted that we drive through these neighborhoods during which she would exclaim at how beautiful the homes and neighborhoods were.

Asbury, the church we joined when we moved from Columbia, was established in 1836 and was started by seventy-five black parishioners, some still slaves, who had broken away from Foundry Methodist Church. Mom remained a loyal supporter of Asbury until her death.

Until I was well into my teens, Mom forced Randy and me to attend Asbury each and every Sunday. And, even when I was quite young, she enforced her rule that I remain fully alert during the service. One Sunday when I continued to nod off during the service and was seemingly unresponsive to her prodding me to remain alert, Mom took me into the church vestibule, lectured me about the importance of being alert during the service, and sharply warned that if I fell asleep again, she would "knock me into the middle of next week." As terrifying, not nearly so, as Mom's threat on other occasions "to knock all of the black off me."

It was very gratifying to Mom that Al and I lived in one of the beautiful homes, indeed an iconic one, that overlooks Rock Creek Park, that she insisted that we drive by after church services. I know she would also be very pleased with our winter home in Naples, Florida.

Our Washington, DC, home in the "Flowers" decorated for Christmas.

Our home in Naples, Florida.

HENRY H. KENNEDY JR.

I did not know any kids in our new neighborhood. I had started playing tennis at the Takoma tennis courts a couple of years earlier, but I mainly had played with the adults there.

One such person was Dave Lifschultz. I met Dave when I had only been playing for a couple of months and went to the tennis courts to watch more experienced players. Dave saw me watching, and after playing himself—sometimes against Alan Centrenbaum, the University of Maryland's number one player—asked if I wanted to hit. I was thrilled and was the beneficiary of some expert teaching by a master tennis tactician for the ensuing two years.

My experience with Dave, Alan Centrenbaum, and other Jews including those at Paul and Coolidge, left a lasting favorable impression on me and accounts for the high regard in which I hold Jewish people and my interest in and support for the nation of Israel.

Shortly after moving to 6600 Seventh Street, in addition to playing tennis, I would go to the recreation center to play Ping-Pong. On the way, I would pass kids playing knockout near a concrete backboard not far from the tennis courts. Knockout, a game created and played by the better players on Takoma's baseball team, the A team, involved a pitcher tossing a hardball to batters who scored when they hit the ball over the backboard to a large grassy area near the swimming pool. I met Robert O'Meally playing knockout. He was to become my best friend and would inspire me to excel academically.

Though I was not a good enough player to play knockout with Bob and the other members of the A team, I was nevertheless befriended by the ball players and was included in the good-natured joshing that was a feature of the interaction between the members of this group. That interaction featured a peculiar verbal game called "joning." The object of joning, also called "counting the dozens" or "sounding," was to say some outlandish insult about someone in the group or a member of his family, often his mother.

We would listen for an insult and would then exclaim, "Sound!" What was said was calculated to get a rise out of the person to whom it was directed and an approving reaction from the other kids who expected the subject of the insult to return an even more outlandish "sound."

Bobby: Hey, Boo I saw your mama last night at the railroad station wearing combat boots.
Boo: Yeah, she was there kicking your mama's ass with those boots.

46

The joning went on for hours with each participant trying to outdo the others in the degree of outrageous insult that could be delivered. The best joners were "Boo" Harris, Charlie ("Cholly") Thomas, and Bobby. I was a mediocre joner at best and was amazed at how creative my new friends were at rhyming insults.

In addition to being close to the Takoma Recreation Center, our home at 6600 Seventh Street was not far from the schools I attended before college.

Whittier Elementary School

After moving to Northwest Washington, DC, I attended Whittier Elementary School at Fifth and Sheridan Street, NW, where I was in Mrs. Colston's sixth grade class, my first integrated educational experience. There, I met Ernest "Chico" Wilson, and—like Bobby—he became a lifelong friend.

Chico was light skinned, very good-looking, and tall and had "good" hair. Chico's father was Dean of Foreign students at Howard University. Chico often displayed a superior exposure to the world, including the world of ideas.

Unlike Bobby, Chico did not excel in sports. He did so academically, however. He always was one of the first to confidently raise his hand in class when Mrs. Colston asked a question and almost always gave the right answer. It is not surprising that Chico went on to Harvard College, earned a MA and PhD in political science from the University of California, Berkeley, before becoming a tenured professor at the University of Maryland and then the dean of the Annenberg School of Communication and Journalism at the University of Southern California.

Chico's father was a fascinating man who had many interesting experiences. He enjoyed regaling Chico, Bobby, and me about the famous people he had occasion to meet and interact with. One of those persons was the actress Elizabeth Taylor whom he met at a conference in Dubai.

Mr. Wilson was also very wise. Chico, Bobby, and I were accepted into every college to which we applied, including our first choices: Harvard for Chico, Stanford for Bobby, and Princeton for me. We went to Chico's house to celebrate. After seeing us thoroughly satisfied with ourselves and our accomplishments, Mr. Wilson said, "Boys, you should be very pleased with getting into these prestigious universities, but always remember that 90 percent of what makes life worth living is to dig and be dug," meaning to love and be loved. Truer words were never spoken.

It was at Whittier that I learned that accomplishment is a sure way to build self-esteem, something many educators and child development experts have determined is essential for constructive adolescent growth. One of my first accomplishments in this regard was to be chosen for Whittier's safety patrol, in which I rose to the rank of second lieutenant.

I was assigned to the busiest corner near the school at Fifth and Sheridan Street, N.W. While I was performing my safety patrol duties, Charles Rich, the school bully, would not follow my directions to cross Fifth Street only in the crosswalk and on a green light. When I admonished him, he told me he would "kick [my] ass" if I reported him to the principal. When I did not back down, we decided to settle the matter by having a fight after school on the playground in back of the school. Charlie was bigger and stronger than me, but—with several of schoolmates looking on—I held my own.

My willingness to take on Charlie earned me creds with my fellow students, even among those who only heard about the fight from others.

One of my most gratifying experiences in recent years was running into Charlie on Sixth Street near the superior court. He was driving a large truck and was delivering office furniture. We embraced, and he told me how proud he was that I had become a judge. It was a truly touching moment.

Paul Junior High

After graduating from Whittier, I went to Paul Junior High School. At Paul, I faced my first significant academic challenge. I had always been a very good student and was recognized as such. When teachers grouped students by ability level within their classes, I was always in the most advanced group. Therefore, neither I nor my parents were pleased when I was placed in Paul's college preparatory track rather than its honors track.

In those days, the DC public school system placed students entering junior high into six tracks: honors, further divided into first and second honors, college preparatory, basic, general, and social adjustment. With the exception of Chico, first honors was populated by white students, as was second honors, except for Bobby and one or two other black students. Those in the college preparatory track were also mostly white, but it had more blacks than in first or second honors. With each descending track, the number of black students increased until the social adjustment track where all the students were black.

Stung by my placement in the college preparatory track and not in the honors track with my best friends, I set about to demonstrate that a mistake had been made and that I too should be in the highest track. To gain placement in honors was an incentive that spawned a study habit that served me well throughout my life.

Based on my experience, I think the tracking system was a good one and should not have been held to be unconstitutional as Judge Skelly Wright did in *Hobson v. Hansen*, 269 F. Supp. 401 (DDC 1967). In *Hobson*, civil rights activist Julius D. Hobson filed a suit against the DC superintendent of schools, Carl F. Hansen, and the District of Columbia Board of Education, alleging that the DC public educational system by employing a tracking system deprived black and poor students of their right to equal educational opportunities on account of race and socioeconomic status. While Judge Wright's opinion convincingly demonstrated that racial animus underlay the tracking system, it seems to me that the tracking system nevertheless made common sense and was an altogether reasonable pedagogical methodology as long as a student like me could move from one track to another.

I had another incentive and influence. When I entered Paul, the student population was very diverse, but the students who were the leaders and most accomplished were the Jewish students. They carried themselves in a way that bespoke a confidence that they would succeed. I found this to be a very attractive quality, one that I did not have and did not see in the vast majority of other students, except for Bobby and Chico.

*My seventh-grade class at Paul Junior High, I am
in the top row, second from the right*

Almost all of the Jewish students had attended the Hebrew Academy on Sixteenth Street before going to Paul. These students included Harry Gildenhorn, Danny Segal, Alan Greene, Steve Kaplan, Marc Spiegel, Gary Bonnet, and Sheila Feinstein. The student who demonstrated the greatest confidence was Harvey Frieshtat. Harvey was two years ahead of me and was everywhere in the school, president of the National Honor Society, secretary of the student council, and parliamentarian of the Future Teachers of America.

Harvey did not know who I was and was totally unaware of how he influenced me. Harvey became a lawyer and, among other accomplishments, rose to the position of managing partner of one of the country's major law firms: McDermott, Will, and Emery.

Endeavoring to emulate the Jewish students and keep pace with Bobby and Chico, I studied with an intensity that I doubt few others could match. I was particularly keen on developing my vocabulary, as early on I discerned that what distinguished the very best students was their ability to manipulate language adequate to the task of expressing what was in their heads and hearts accurately and with nuance. I developed these skills so that by the time I was in eighth grade, I was placed in honors. In ninth grade, my classmates voted me most likely to succeed.

Camp Atwater

Equally as important to my development as the time during the school year at Paul Junior High were the six weeks during the summer months that I spent at Camp Atwater. Camp Atwater is a summer camp in North Brookfield, Massachusetts. It was founded in 1921 by Dr. William Newberry and named in honor of Dr. David Fisher Atwater. Located on the shores of Lake Lashaway on property donated by Mary Atwater, the daughter of Dr. Atwater, Camp Atwater was established to provide a summer recreational experience for African American youth at a time when summer camps were generally racially segregated or did not exist for black children. The camp catered primarily to middle- and upper-class African American boys and drew attendees from up and down the Atlantic Coast and a few from the Midwest. The name for the camp and its location are appropriate for the bucolic, peaceful, and woodsy setting of this beautiful place.

My parents learned of Camp Atwater from the parents of Shuford Hill, a youngster who had attended the camp for several summers. Shuford, an outstanding track athlete who attended Bishop J. O'Connell High School in suburban Virginia, had enjoyed Camp Atwater immensely. As it turned out, I did too.

The boy's session of the Atwater camp season lasted from June to the latter part of July. Except for the first time when I was driven to Camp Atwater by my parents, I traveled to camp by train and bus, departing on a train from Union Station in Washington, D.C. to Worcester, Massachusetts, and from there by bus to North Brookfield where my brother and I, the two summers he attended, were met by a Camp Atwater staffer who drove us to the camp. Looking back on my camp experiences, I am surprised that my parents let me travel such a distance alone. I suspect they early on wanted to teach me to be self-sufficient.

The activities provided by Camp Atwater were done in a disciplined manner. They effectively taught important life lessons. Each day started at 7 a.m. with campers and counselors surrounding the flagpole located near the banks of Lake Lashaway and saluting the raising of the flag to reveille. The camp director was Mr. Dickerson, a straight arrow from Philadelphia who, dressed in starched, creased khaki pants and a white T-shirt, stood ramrod straight and led the salute and recitation of the Pledge of Allegiance with his right hand over his heart. For Mr. D, this obviously was not mere ritual but an important and fitting way to start the day by expressing patriotism.

After the flag was raised, campers assembled in the dining hall where we were treated to all the healthy breakfast foods we could eat. Breakfast lasted half an hour after which the campers returned to their huts and cleaned them in preparation for Mr. D's daily inspection.

Counselors Dennis Hightower and Ronald Flowers and campers assigned to Pines Hut. I am in the second row, third from the right.

The cleaning of the huts consisted of each camper making his bed so that the "hospital" corners were just so, the sheets were tight, and just the right amount of the sheets on the bed peeked out from each bed's blanket. The floors and front porch of the hut were swept each day. The dirt in front of the porch of each hut was raked so that the dirt showed the strokes of the rake's tongs. Early on, each camper learned that the inspection of the huts was to be taken seriously and that it was a very worthy effort to earn the plaque that was given for the cleanest and best-maintained hut at the end of the camp season, an accomplishment to be cherished as much as being awarded any other plaque given during the season-ending awards ceremony.

Following inspection, each camper went to his first assigned camp activity. Mine each season was swimming, an activity in which each camper was required to participate. Many of the campers dreaded swimming early in the morning because typically the temperature of the water in Lake Lashaway at that time of the day was quite chilly with the temperature of the air being no more than fifty or fifty-five degrees. I never felt that way as I was accustomed to waking early in the morning and getting into the chilly water of the pool at the YMCA when I practiced back home in DC for the swim team.

Each camper was evaluated within the first week of camp for his swimming proficiency. Depending upon one's ability, a camper was given either a white, blue, or red swim cap, which he was required to wear anytime he participated in an activity in the lake. The most proficient swimmers were given a white cap, which was earned by swimming a significant distance, about 150 yards, toward the island that was in the middle of the lake.

The pier at Camp Atwater and the island in the middle of Lake Lashaway.

Campers with a white cap could swim anywhere in the lake they wanted, including to the island. Campers with a blue cap could swim in an area just outside the pier that was enclosed by a thick rope and buoys. Campers with a red cap were restricted to an area bound by a metal pier in which the water was no more than three or four feet deep.

I easily met the requirements for a white cap and distinguished myself as a swimmer. During my last two camp seasons, I was assigned lifeguard duties, which included being one of two persons in a rowboat who proceeded in front of campers trying to earn their white cap. In the summer of 1962, I was in the back of a rowboat watching a camper swimming toward the island when he began to flail his arms and then suddenly sank into Lake Lashaway's dark waters. I immediately dove into the water but had trouble locating the distressed swimmer. When I saw air bubbles in the murky water, I grabbed the dark figure that was nearby and brought it to the surface where the camper was quickly hauled into the boat and successfully given CPR.

Aside from the splendid activities offered by the camp, for me, the ingredient that made Camp Atwater most special was its counselors. My most memorable counselor was my first, Dennis Hightower, the counselor of Pines Hut. Dennis was a student at Howard University and was a thoroughly engaging young man who, perceived through the eyes of a twelve-year-old, looked to be very tall. In reality he was short, about five foot four, as I learned many years later when I reconnected with him. I was enthralled with the sophistication and worldliness he displayed in various ways. For example, I loved to overhear his conversations at night with our assistant counselor, Ronald Flowers, also a Howard University student, with whom he shared a bunk bed at the front of our hut. They talked knowingly about dating and having sex with girls. It seemed that they were both successful in that department and made me want to have sex even more than I did already.

One of the most enjoyable activities instituted by Dennis and Ron was done whenever any camper got out of line. When this happened, all the campers in the hut were required to take the mattresses off their beds and place them along the walls of the hut. The campers then took their metal bed frames outside, leaving an empty hut except for the mattresses that lined the walls. The campers, including those who had nothing to do with the offending conduct, were then repeatedly picked up by Dennis and Ron and forcefully thrown against the walls of the hut where the mattresses softened their impact.

Looking back, I shudder at how dangerous this was, but I recall this activity with immense pleasure. So it was that campers deliberately did something to instigate this "discipline."

After college and his days as a camp counselor at Camp Atwater, Dennis went on to distinguish himself in the military, business, and government. Following his graduation from Howard University, Dennis completed the US Army Ranger School and US Army Airborne School. He served in Vietnam rising to the rank of major at age twenty-seven. After his military service, he joined Xerox, and two years later, he studied at Harvard and earned his MBA. Following Harvard Business School, he was a senior associate/engagement manager at McKinsey & Company, vice president and general manager of General Electric's lighting business in Mexico, vice president of corporate strategy at Mattel, and managing director at Russell Reynolds Associates. In 1987, he was recruited by the Walt Disney Company, where he served as president of Disney Consumer Products for Europe, the Middle East, and Africa, based in Paris and later as president of Walt Disney Television and Telecommunications, then Disney's largest division. When Dennis retired from the Walt Disney Company, he was among the six highest-ranking African American executives in corporate America. He became President Obama's Deputy Secretary of Commerce in 2009.

To me, everything about Camp Atwater was perfect, including the various sports activities the camp offered, several in which I excelled. At the end of the camp season, there was a competition for each activity in which most campers competed, hoping to win a coveted wooden trophy carved by "Box" James, a most engaging senior counselor. Every year I attended, I won the tennis tournament, the Ping-Pong tournament, and several events in the swim meet, often breaking the camp record, which stood for many years.

Plaques made out of wood by "Box" James and presented to the winners of Camp Atwater's competitions.

Because I loved Camp Atwater so much, I persuaded Bobby and Chico to attend. I was disappointed when they both did not enjoy the experience at all. I perceived that they thought all the esprit de corps fostered by the camp and that I embraced and found so gratifying was corny and juvenile.

The camp season always ended with a bonfire and the telling of the story of Bigfoot. Soon after arriving at Camp Atwater, campers would hear snippets of a tale of a half-human, half-animal creature that looked like a big hairy bear with a hairy human face. Camp administrators told the campers Bigfoot was known to devour small animals and youngsters and that they were relieved that Bigfoot had not made an appearance at Camp Atwater for several seasons.

The final night of each camp season found campers sitting around a large bonfire at the edge of the deep dark woods that surrounded the camp. Box James or Mr. D, both master storytellers, told the complete story of Bigfoot in excruciating detail so that he came alive. The storyteller told such details as to why Bigfoot was so angry and ferocious—he was mistreated as a child by his parents who were scientists and abandoned him when an experiment on him went bad—his size—at last sighting about six foot six—and his siblings, two whom he killed and ate. The evening ended with a heartfelt wish for the campers to have safe travel to their respective homes.

Immediately after the gathering was dismissed, a blood-curdling scream came from the woods and a Big Foot impersonator wearing a horrific furry costume and mask stormed from the woods toward the younger campers! This induced panic, and the campers ran for their lives from the terror. It was something to experience, and it was a bit too much for the younger ones. Several of them broke into tears.

I attended Camp Atwater four summers in a row and never tired of this season-ending tradition—even when I knew precisely what would happen.

One of the proudest times in my life was the camp season when I won Camp Atwater's Best All-Around award. As the name suggests, this award was given to the camper who excelled in every aspect of camp life, sports, camaraderie, and leadership. That summer, as during other camp seasons, I had won several swimming events at the swim meet, breaking the camp record in two of the events, and the tennis and table tennis tournaments. I also gave a performance at the talent show where I did a rousing rendition of Jerry Lee Lewis's "Great Balls of Fire," a song I had learned years before and had performed in my third grade class at Turner Elementary School. I brought the house down with my over-the-top performance that included banging the keys of the piano with my feet as Jerry Lee was famous for doing.

I have been appointed by the Attorney General of the United States as an Assistant United States Attorney, to three judicial posts, two by presidents of the United States, and a trustee of Princeton University, but none rival winning Camp Atwater's Best All-Around award.

Also unrivaled for me in a completely different sphere, an adolescent boy whose hormones were raging, was the warm summer night toward the camp season's end when I walked Diane Williams, the daughter of the camp nurse, to her house, which was located at the top of the hill near the edge of the camp. In the front yard, under a large birch tree, I kissed her. It was so very sweet and, to me, very sensual.

All these years later, I still remember the Camp Atwater song, which was sung with gusto at every significant camp event:

Shout for Camp Atwater long may she live; nestled under the birches truth and light she gives; blue and white are flowing, so answer her call, shout for Camp Atwater the best camp of all!

Coolidge High School

The graduates of Paul Junior High who stayed in the public school system went to Calvin Coolidge High School, located at Fifth and Tuckerman Streets, NW, directly across the street from Whittier Elementary. Chico did not go to Coolidge because he received a prestigious appointment to attend the National Page School.

By the time I entered Coolidge, the number of white students there had decreased dramatically from the years before, a result of white flight, a very apt description of the phenomenon of white families starting in the 1950s to leave the neighborhoods in which they had lived for years when black families like mine started to become their neighbors.

Real estate brokers engaged in "blockbusting." Brokers would exploit the fear of middle-class white residents by buying their properties below cost and reselling to blacks at a large profit. White flight and blockbusting began in the 1950s and continued until at least the 1970s.

I entered Coolidge in September 1963. Two months later, on November 22, President John F. Kennedy was assassinated—and my sister, Angela, was born. With the birth of Angela, I became a big brother again, but given the wide difference in our ages, sixteen years, I treated her more like a daughter than a sister. I became protective of her, a natural reaction for me for this wonderful addition to our family but also an expected attitude given the expectations of my father. Of course, I would always want to do what was expected of me by my father, particularly as it concerned support of family, something my father expected of any man worthy of being called one.

The student body at Coolidge still was relatively racially and ethnically diverse when I started there. By 1966, however, the year I graduated, my class of approximately four hundred students was comprised of about 20 percent white students, 70 percent black, with a smattering of first-generation immigrants whose parents were born in Asia, the Caribbean, or Africa. At school, the students of different races got along very well. However, there was very little interracial contact outside of school.

My fellow students at Coolidge High were generally well-behaved and desirous of getting ahead. I came to like many of them very much and had many friends, including the members of Omicron Upsilon Phi, the high school fraternity to which I belonged, and the Upsilon's rivals, the Royals. Other classmates I came to particularly like were Percy Luney, who was a high-ranking officer in the cadets and became among other accomplishments, the dean of the National Judicial College in Reno, Nevada, Rodney Ellis, an outstanding physician, Donna Bassin, whose parents owned an upscale restaurant, Bassins, in downtown DC, Michael Snipes, a superb football player who was always good-natured and always wore a smile, Theresa Lewis, who never seeking recognition for herself always worked behind the scenes to make school projects work, Donna Williams, the secretary of the class whose sister I kissed at Camp Atwater, Diane Bumbry and Donna Royster, two very cute cheerleaders who embodied school spirit, Judith Specter and Sandra Wender, who on the first day of school predicted that I would become class president, Chris Dixon, the class vice president, James Coley and Charles Green, whom I knew from Whittier Elementary, James Chandler, whose father headed the Boy Scout troop in which I participated when I was at Whittier, Alex Clifton, a neighbor I see fairly often these days, Harry Bass, a superb singer, Alexandra Mallus, the class valedictorian, Elizabeth Lindsay, Norma Paper, whom I'll always remember for her performance in Li'l Abner and her friend Barbara Sargovitz, and Jimille Shorter, my high school girlfriend and simply a thoroughly good person.

While I had a lot of friends I had to campaign hard to become senior class president. My opponent, Pearl Williams, was pretty and popular. To offset Pearl's advantages, I asked the Simmons twins, Frank and Perry, both star football players, to be my campaign managers. Realizing that the speech at the assembly held to give the candidates an opportunity to tell the members of the senior class why they should vote for a particular candidate would be important, I devoted a great deal of time to crafting my campaign speech.

With the assistance of Bob O'Meally I wrote a speech that while short on substance as to what I would do as class president was long on appeal to the collective ego of the members of the class. Thus, with a seasoned politician's vigor and without shame, I told my classmates that I would be honored to represent them, undoubtedly members of the best class that had ever graced the hallways and grounds of Coolidge High School. I boomed that I intended no disrespect to the many classes that had preceded ours, such as the "satisfying class of '65" or the "thoroughly good class of '64," but that I would be honored to lead the "supercalifragilisticexpealidocious class of 1966!"

This over-the-top reference to a verse in a song performed in a then very popular film, *Mary Poppins*, brought the house down. I won the election for class president going away and since have declared myself, with the good-natured consent of my classmates, to be president for life, "mine or yours, whichever comes later."

Coolidge's teachers and administrators were much less diverse than the student body. In 1966, the year I graduated, there were eleven African American teachers and administrators out of a total of seventy. The principal was Cedric O. Reynolds, a middle-aged white man with an unattractive white fringe of hair encircling his balding head. Except for the one time he visited one of the planning meetings for the C-Club dance, an annual dance that took place in the gymnasium, Mr. Reynolds was rarely seen outside his office.

At a C-Club meeting, a meeting of the Coolidge varsity athletes entitled to wear letter jackets and sweaters, Principal Reynolds unexpectedly dropped in on the meeting and proclaimed that at the dance there would be no "dry humping." We all knew what he was referring to.

"Dry humping," which we called "grinding," was a style of slow dancing in basement house parties. It would start whenever a slow record was played. A boy would approach a girl and, without saying a word, hold out his hand. The girl understood this to be an invitation to dance. If the girl took his hand, the two would go on the dance floor and would begin to grind. The grind involved the boy placing both of his arms over the arms of the girl, hugging her very close to him, inserting his leg between her thighs, and initiating a slow back-and-forth movement.

The slow songs of the day were perfect for grinding, including "Ooh Baby Baby" by Smokey Robinson and the Miracles, "Slow Drag" by the Intruders, "Who's Lovin' You," "Would I Love You," and "Where Did You Go" by the Four Tops, "Love Won't Let Me Wait" by Major Harris, "La-La

Means I Love You" and "Didn't I Blow Your Mind This Time" by the Delfonics, "Our Day Will Come" by Ruby and the Romantics, and "The Bells" by the Originals.

Grinding was wonderfully erotic, so much so that boys sometimes would ejaculate on the dance floor and stain their pants. For this reason, most boys wore dark pants that would conceal any stain they would secrete while grinding. Some boys also wore jockstraps to help conceal their erections.

It was at one of those parties that I met Virginia "Ginger" Brown, a girl Bobby knew from the church they both attended, Saint Luke's Episcopal Church, the first separate "colored" Episcopal church in the District of Columbia organized in 1873 by Dr. Alexander Crumwell. Bobby "liked" Ginger, and the two had gone on group trips sponsored by the church. When Bobby discerned that I was attracted to her, he gave me the green light to "talk" to her.

I was truly smitten by Ginger. She was attractive, a great dancer, smart, and quick-witted. We "went together" for about a year during which I was her escort to the debutante ball, an affair known by the DC black elite as the Cotillion, an event that was sponsored by the exclusive Girlfriends social club. Recently, I learned from Ginger that it was her mother, Sarah Brown, who insisted that Ginger invite me to be her escort. The coming-out also involved weekly parties over the course of six weeks preceding the ball to which the debutantes would be taken by their escorts.

In the fall of 1965, the debutantes and their escorts waltzed at the Cotillion to a rendition of "Fly Me to the Moon" performed by Bobby Felder and the Blue Notes at the Washington Hilton Hotel.

Ginger is the daughter of Dillard Houston Brown Jr., the ninth Episcopalian Missionary Bishop of Liberia, who lived there the entire time I dated her. Ginger's mother, Sarah, was a very sweet lady who loved her husband very much and doted on Ginger.

Ginger attended the upscale National Cathedral School for Girls (NCS). One of her classmates was Luci Johnson, the younger daughter of President Lyndon Johnson. Luci, while rhythmically challenged, enthusiastically danced the Watusi, a popular dance of the times, at the NCS prom to which I escorted Ginger.

I met Bishop Brown only once. Ginger, who loved and greatly admired her father, brought him to my house when he was visiting the United States. We talked briefly outside on the front porch. Short and dark skinned, Bishop Brown exuded confidence and gravitas. When he spoke, his voice sounded like it rose from the depths of the earth, very deep with a pleasant but serious timbre. We did little more than exchange pleasantries while Ginger looked on with delight as I tried to maintain my cool while speaking with her father. Ginger went on to become an Episcopalian minister and became the ninth rector of Saint Luke's in 1999.

Tragically, Ginger's father was shot to death in his office on November 19, 1969, in Monrovia, Liberia, when he went to the aid of a secretary, Patricia Lewis, who was accosted in an outer office of the Chase Manhattan office building where he maintained his offices. The gunman was identified as a young student and instructor at an Episcopal school in Liberia.

It was during high school that I was most active in Jack and Jill, an African American mother's club, which gives the children of the black professional class an opportunity to socialize with one another. And socialize we did at the monthly activities planned and executed by our mothers. These activities were varied—from learning to dance the Charleston and the cha-cha, a most memorable activity planned by Yetta Galiber, a community activist whose husband was a dentist and the mother of two sons and a daughter, to volunteering at local shelters, to attending a weekend trip to the Penn Relays, a national track meet in Philadelphia.

At a party in Philadelphia, during a Jack-and-Jill trip to the Penn Relays, I gathered my nerves and asked the then queen of Jack and Jill, Brenda Adams, to dance. Brenda, the daughter of a physician, was drop-dead beautiful and quite stylish, wearing a pink leather miniskirt, matching leather vest, and stiletto high-heeled patent leather boots. And could she dance! Seeing her dancing to "Shake a Tail Feather" is a visual every adolescent boy should experience at least once!

The party in Philadelphia was very much like the house parties in Washington, which typically were held on a Friday or Saturday night in the basement of a large house. The lighting was provided by no more than two dim blue light bulbs, hence the name we gave these parties in later years, "blue lights in the basement." The host provided light fare to eat: potato chips, onion dip, soda, and sometimes meatballs. Of course, the host made sure that he or she had the most recent popular records on 45 rpm discs and gave thought to the sequence in which they were played.

The party always started with a succession of upbeat, fast dance tunes that brought all in attendance to the dance floor. Thus, the party would typically start with "Do You Love Me" and "First I look at the Purse" by the Contours, "Shake a Tail Feather" by the Five Dutones, and "Papa's Got a Brand-New Bag (one and two)" by James Brown, "the hardest-working man in show business." It was at this stage in the evening when you brought your best moves to the dance floor. Though no one said it, both the boys and girls were in competition to see who had the sexiest and fastest spins or the most intricate turns while hand dancing.

Hand dancing as done by black teenagers in DC involved complicated turns that had the girl turning in each direction to return to a position facing the boy who, with just a tap on her palm, would send her spinning again in the opposite direction. It was remarkable that even though many times the boy and girl had never danced with each other before, they could synchronize their moves without a hitch.

One's clothing at these parties was important. The cool boys wore gabardine pants, Ban-Lon shirts, and Footjoy shoes or desert boots. The girls wore A-line skirts, tight strapless blouses, and "slingshots"—or "sixteen" shoes, so named because they cost sixteen dollars.

One's attitude at the parties was also vitally important. The boys attempted to convey a sense of confidence and insouciance that was meant to communicate "both you and I know I am cool, and of course you want me to ask you to dance." The girls too adopted an air of nonchalance and strived to communicate "in your wildest dreams, you never thought you'd get this close to somebody as *phat* (good-looking) as I am. You know you want to at least get close to it."

After the succession of fast records, the slow records were played. At that point in the party, the boys made their big moves. They might have danced fast with a girl to whom they had little attraction, but with "Ooh Baby Baby" "Love Won't Let Me Wait" or "I Wanna Know Your Name" spinning on the turntable, the boys reached out for the girls they had been fantasizing about all week.

My main extracurricular activity at Coolidge High School was playing tennis. The number three player on the team my first year at Coolidge was Alan Green. Alan is Jewish and lived on Aspen Street, three blocks from my house and the same distance from the tennis courts. Alan and I often practiced together and became good friends. He was smart, knowledgeable about political matters, and a very good pianist. Alan introduced me to jazz music. One day after tennis practice, he excitedly invited me to his house. When we got there, we went to his bedroom where he played "The Girl from Ipanema" by Stan Getz and Astrud Gilberto on his stereo. Alan simply loved it and insisted that I listen to it as he played it over and over again. It came to be one of my favorite songs too. In the spring of 2013, I was delighted to visit the restaurant where the song was composed in Rio de Janeiro, Brazil.

Alan became a lifelong friend whose friendship was cemented in later years as we supported each other in confronting the mental illness, depression, with which we both had been afflicted. Like me, Alan was beset by this insidious disease after he reached adulthood. Particularly during my last episode of depression, when Alan would come to Washington from New York, we would go out for lunch or coffee to talk about our condition and its treatment. At the time, Alan was in remission and was able to listen and talk with me knowledgeably and compassionately about what I was going through. We talked about the necessity of never losing hope that we would emerge from the darkness and sadness. We also talked about our therapists and the talk therapy that was part of our treatment. We also discussed the value of the cocktail of medications the psychiatrists prescribed for us and concluded that the practice of psychiatry was much more art than science and lamented the uncertainty that this proposition meant for us.

The diverse group of students at Coolidge got along well together in school, on the various sports teams, and during other extracurricular activities. With notable exceptions, however, there was very little socializing together away from school. This lack of social integration was the reason for the creation of a neighborhood group called Neighbors, Inc., the brainchild of Marvin Caplan.

When schools were desegregated in Washington in 1954, there was white flight to the suburbs. The flight was encouraged by unscrupulous real estate agents who attempted to grab houses at rock-bottom prices by falsely warning residents that their real estate values would decline or that schools would be degraded. The methods were many, but they often included renting small houses to large families and telling neighbors the families had purchased the house.

Neighbors, Inc. responded with a two-pronged program. It found reputable real estate agents who would sell to all home buyers—black and white—without discrimination. It made sure white couples were not steered away from the neighborhood. It reached out to members of the new Kennedy administration and the diplomatic community to interest them in the neighborhood. It worked tirelessly to support local school programs, including nationally renowned events like the Annual Art and Book Festival, which was held at Coolidge High School, and the annual Valentine's dance with its "Love Your Neighbor" theme. These events stimulated media interest, excitement, and a constant stream of willing buyers to the community.

When there was social interaction in school between black and white students, some of the older teachers took exception. Eileen Barder was a cute Jewish girl who, like me and most of the students at Coolidge, was aware of Virginia Quick's racial animus. Quick taught Latin, was a spinster, and was older than most of the other teachers. To aggravate her, Eileen and I decided to hold hands while switching class. In those days, while students were changing classes, teachers would stand in the hall outside their classrooms to monitor them. When Eileen and I walked past Quick holding hands, she curled her bony index finger and curtly summoned Eileen. Eileen complied, and when Quick saw the Star of David hanging from a chain around Eileen's neck, Quick tossed it aside, and with a voice brimming with disgust, she said, "I should have known."

News of this incident got around the school and provided the backdrop for one of my most gratifying experiences. Quick was the teacher in charge of the National Honor Society. Both Eileen and I had earned grades that qualified us for induction into the society, but Quick had the ultimate authority to decide who would be inducted. It became a matter of substantial interest in the school whether Quick would block Eileen's and my induction into the society at the induction ceremony that was held in the school's auditorium.

I was very concerned that Quick would block my induction and deprive me of a credit that would be extremely valuable for my college applications. I know that Eileen was concerned too, though she was in a grade behind me and was not thinking of college applications yet.

When the time for the induction ceremony came, the auditorium was full, something that did not happen often for activities other than the talent show. When each name was called, the new inductee walked to the stage. There was polite applause acknowledging the inductee's accomplishment. When Eileen's and my names were called, the students stood as one and delivered a thunderous ovation. The unmistakable message being sent was that racism and anti-Semitism would no longer be tolerated at Coolidge.

Coolidge had many very fine teachers who were dedicated to their craft and interested in the development of their charges as people and in promoting good race relations at the school. In the 1960s, race matters were at the center of various concerns and social policy in the country. Teachers like Helen Levinson, who taught French and journalism, Lyn McClain, who headed Coolidge's music department and was founder of the city-wide high school orchestra, Georgia Popps, and Ann Smith who taught social studies, Helena Lamberth, who taught business education, and Leonard Himes, the physics teacher and tennis coach, were superb—and I believe as good as any teachers anywhere.

Mr. Himes did not teach stroke production or tennis strategy. However, he went out of his way to provide our team competition against prestigious private schools in the area—and as far away as Pennsylvania and Virginia. It was through my travels with the tennis team that I saw education facilities at upscale private schools like Saint Albans in Washington, the

Woodberry Forest School in Virginia, and the Mercersburg Academy in Pennsylvania.

In tenth grade, I did not do well against the players at these schools. They all had classic games and beat me handily. However, during the summer of 1965, I improved considerably so that in my last year I was unbeaten in high school league competition and was ranked number one in DC.

My junior year, I played a memorable match against the number one player at Saint Albans. I won handily and played so well that Allie Ritzenberg, Saint Albans's legendary coach, offered me a tennis scholarship to attend and play for Saint Albans. I declined, giving some explanation, but not the truthful one, for turning down his offer. Instead, I told Allie that I had a younger brother who was a good tennis player who would make good use of a scholarship to Saint Albans.

The truth was that since the first semester of my junior year, I was "going with" Jimille Shorter, a classmate at Coolidge, and I was not about to risk jeopardizing my relationship with her by going to another school. Jimille was very pretty and played the cello in the DC Youth Orchestra that practiced at Coolidge. Jimille had a relationship with Xavier Beard who was a year ahead of us at Coolidge and had graduated. I knew that she loved him. I was content, however, with being her on-the-scene boyfriend only, willing to play second fiddle given my immense affection and admiration for her.

Jimille sadly developed multiple sclerosis shortly after graduating from Catholic University and marrying Xavier. She confronted her illness with courage, never complained, had a daughter to whom she was devoted, and lived a wonderful, though shortened, life with the man she had loved since Coolidge High School. Jimille, I salute you. Rest in peace, my dear friend.

My match against St. Albans' number one player was very satisfying and consequential for me and my family, but it was not my most gratifying tennis match during my high school years. I had three others. Coolidge was located in Upper Northwest Washington, east of Rock Creek Park, and had had a tennis team for years. Each year it participated in the DC Public Schools league play and almost always lost the decisive match against Woodrow Wilson High School, a school then comprised mostly of white students. Wilson was located in the more affluent part of the city west of Rock Creek Park in Northwest Washington and typically fielded teams whose players played and had been taught at the country clubs.

In my junior year, the championship match was played at the tennis courts near Coolidge at the Takoma Recreation Center. The deciding match came down to a doubles match, pitting the Kawakami brothers, Chris and Clark, two very good Asian American players, against me and Robert Freeman, a good black player who had injured his leg and was playing with it heavily bandaged.

We split the first two sets of the match, and Bob and I got behind in the third. Bob played with courage and tremendous pain, and with every shot, he became less and less mobile. In order to have any chance of winning, we decided I would have to play a high-risk game. I did just that, poaching with abandon on Robert's serve, running around my backhand on the return of serve, teeing off on it with a massive forehand, or chipping the return and rushing the net. We won in a squeaker as the sun was setting on a perfect spring evening. I was as proud of that win as any during my young tennis career.

Today, Robert is a well-regarded artist who is much admired for his bold and colorful brushwork and paintings of well-heeled African Americans at sophisticated social gatherings. I have gone to several exhibits of his paintings in DC and was most pleased recently to purchase two of them.

Another very satisfying tennis match occurred during the summer of 1965. That summer I had been selected to participate in the American Tennis Association's junior development program. The American Tennis Association, the oldest African American sports organization in the United States, was conceived when the United States Lawn Tennis Association issued a policy statement formally barring African American tennis players from its tournaments. The ATA was born when representatives from more than a dozen black tennis clubs met in Washington on November 30, 1916.

The ATA's junior development program was conceived and operated by Dr. Robert Walter Johnson, an African American physician who had been a standout football player at Lincoln University in Lancaster, Pennsylvania, the United States' first degree-granting historically black university. Dr. Johnson's dazzling speed as a halfback, who was known for eluding the grasp of defenders by "whirling" away from them when they attempted to tackle him, earned him the nickname Whirlwind. After finishing medical school at Meharry in Nashville, Tennessee, Dr. Johnson became a civil rights leader who became the first African American physician to receive practice rights at Lynchburg General Hospital in Virginia.

He also became extremely interested in tennis. Every year, Doc would identify the most talented black junior players in the country and invite them to train in his program with the hope that they could be groomed to compete successfully in national USLTA tournaments, almost all of which were held at private tennis clubs. The program was located in Lynchburg, Virginia, at Dr. Johnson's home on Pierce Street, which had one clay court in the backyard.

I was delighted to be selected by Dr. Johnson to participate in the junior development program. In June, shortly after the end of the school year, I quit my job at McDonald's, where I was the "shake man," and boarded a Greyhound bus to Lynchburg.

Doc had to persuade tournament directors and those in charge of the USLTA to permit his black charges to compete. One of those players was Althea Gibson. She was the first black athlete to cross the color line of international tennis. In 1956, she became the first person of color to win a Grand Slam title: the French Open. The following year, she won both Wimbledon and the US Nationals (the precursor of the US Open), won both again in 1958, and was voted Female Athlete of the Year by the Associated Press in both years. In all, she won eleven Grand Slam tournaments, including six doubles titles.

Another African American tennis player mentored by Dr. Johnson was Arthur Ashe. First noticed and taught by Ronald Charity in Richmond and identified as a youngster with immense talent, Ashe was the first black player selected to the United States Davis Cup team and the only black man ever to win the singles title at Wimbledon, the US Open, and the Australian Open.

In the summer of 1965, the ATA National Junior Championships were held at North Carolina A&T College in Greensboro. There was only one white player in the tournament. He was very good, and with every round he won, handily beating some very good black players, the buzz got louder regarding how unfortunate it would be if the only white player in the black championships was to win it.

I played the white kid in the semifinal round. Our match was a battle royal in sweltering heat and humidity on an August afternoon in front of all the other participants. Refusing to give up on any shot, we both gave it our all, each falling several times on the red clay, scraping our knees so badly that they bled. We split sets and were tied deep in the third when I lost consciousness and fell hard to the court. When I regained consciousness, Dr. Johnson was leaning over me. I looked up into his angular jet-black face. He said only four words: "Get up and win." I did, defeating my opponent in three grueling sets. I was told by onlookers that when I fell to the ground, Doc ran onto the courts with a black medical bag, pulled down my shorts, and injected something in my butt cheek. Among the ATA juniors, this win won me the moniker "White Boy Beater."

*My opponent and me after our semifinal match in July 1965
at the ATA Junior National Championships at North Carolina
A&T in Greensboro. Note the red clay stains on our shirts.*

I owed my selection to the ATA junior development program to two matches I played in the spring of 1965 that caught Dr. Johnson's attention. At a major tournament held at a prestigious private school, the Sidwell Friends School in Washington, I played Bobby Goeltz in the semifinal round. Goeltz attended Landon, a private school for boys, in Chevy Chase, Maryland. He was one of the best high school players in the country and was the reigning interscholastic champion. He was the only player besides Arthur Ashe to win the National Interscholastic Championships three years in a row and went on to become Princeton's number one player. I lost to Goeltz in the semifinal round 7–5, 7–5 in a very tight match.

My other credential for Dr. Johnson's elite program was my win over Harold Solomon in a tournament at the Edgemoor Club in Bethesda, Maryland. Solomon was three years younger than me, but he had won the national 14s championships in Kalamazoo, Michigan, and had been identified as an up-and-coming young player who was destined to distinguish himself on the world stage. Harold learned the game when he was five years old. My match with him was highly anticipated among the youngsters who competed in the DC metropolitan area. Harold had won many of the junior tournaments in the area and had gained a national reputation with his unorthodox game, which featured a two-handed backhand and a remarkable ability to play a focused and error-free game. I too had won some tournaments, all of them local, and I was known for my American twist serve and hard-penetrating forehand. The tennis crowd was anxious to see how the two of us would match up.

Our hard-fought match was played in front of onlookers including my father and Harold's father, Leonard. I won in three sets, primarily on the strength of my serve and forehand. The serve, which I developed after many hours of practice at the courts at Takoma, was executed by my bending my legs and back until my back was almost parallel to the ground and then exploding upward to the ball thrown high over my left shoulder. At contact, if the ball is visualized as a clock, was struck at seven o'clock. This action produced a tremendous amount of torque and spin that was imparted to the ball, causing it to jump sideways when it hit in the service box. The ball bounced high to Harold's two-handed backhand, out of his strike zone. This frequently resulted in a weak service return to my forehand, which I hit with tremendous velocity and topspin to either corner.

I was glad to that my father was there to see me win the match against Harold. For three or four days after the match, Harold's father picked me up at my house and drove me to Indian Springs Country Club where Harold was coached and practiced. I did nothing but hit my American twist serve to Harold.

That serve earned me an offer of a four-year scholarship to Ohio Wesleyan University. In the fall of 1965, I was invited to Ohio Wesleyan for a try out. I was playing Ohio Wesleyan's top player when I hit a serve that hit a pebble, jumped over my opponent's head, and then spiraled over the fence. I was made an offer for a four-year tennis scholarship on the spot.

Harold went on to have a phenomenal career as a professional tennis player. He ranked in the top ten in the world for several years, represented the United States in Davis Cup competition, and he reached the finals of the French Open in 1976 where he lost to Adriano Pennata, Italy's top player, in four sets. His best year was in 1980, and his win-loss record was 64–23. He also appeared in *Playgirl*'s list of the ten sexiest men that year.

As impressive as Harold's achievements were as a tennis player, they were no more impressive than his efforts to advance racial justice, when he was only fourteen years old, before he became rich and famous. In 1966, the Middle Atlantic section of the United States Lawn Tennis Association championships were held at the Hermitage Country Club, not far from Richmond, Virginia. Harold had been distinguishing himself in national tournaments, but this sectional championship was important to him as well. Another very good player from the Middle Atlantic section was Weldon Rogers, a black youngster who was the son of civil rights leader and minister, Jefferson Rogers. When Weldon and his father arrived at the tournament site, they were told that Weldon would be able to compete in the tournament, but he would have to play his matches on the nearby public tennis courts because the club would not permit blacks to play on the courts there. Learning of this, Harold and his father led a walkout of the tournament that was joined by several players from the Middle Atlantic section.

The other players in Dr. Johnson's program during the summer of 1965, all of whom had participated in the program during previous summers, were Luis Glass, Lenward Simpson, Robert Binns, Bonnie Logan, and Tina Watanabe. Luis Glass was from Jackson Heights, New York, and was attending the Deerfield Academy in Deerfield, Massachusetts. He was the most talented among us. Luis was very personable, about six foot two, lean, and very handsome. He had all the shots, but he had an exceptionally good serve and backhand, which he hit with tremendous power and spin.

In 1965, Luis earned a scholarship to UCLA where he was 9–0 playing singles as a freshman. By the end of his freshman year, he lost his scholarship, left school, entered the army, and served in Vietnam. He spent a year as a medic, administering to wounded soldiers. When he returned, he attended Hampton Institute, where he was twice named All-American in singles.

Lenward Simpson is from Wilmington, North Carolina. He was a big guy and had a fearsome demeanor and wicked topspin forehand. Lenward and Luis competed in the boys National Championships in Kalamazoo. They teamed in doubles and played Stan Smith and Bob Lutz in the tournament's semifinal round where they lost in five sets. Both Lutz and Smith became professional tennis players, and Smith became the nation's number one player and was inducted into the International Tennis Hall of Fame. At fifteen, Lenward was the youngest male ever to compete in World Team Tennis, and he was the first African American to do so. He was inducted into the North Carolina Tennis Hall of Fame in 2011.

Robert Binns is a slightly built player from Cleveland, Ohio, who was very fleet afoot with an amazingly versatile two-handed backhand. He was a standout player at John Hay High School in Cleveland and went on to play varsity tennis at Columbia University.

Bonnie Logan was from Durham, North Carolina, and she was

recognized as a very gifted player with enormous potential. She dominated the American Tennis Association tournaments during the 1960s, including capturing seven consecutive ATA women's singles titles (1964–1970). Bonnie went to Morgan State University in Baltimore, and she petitioned to join the men's tennis team. Her petition was granted. She went on to play number two for the team and won the number two flight in the Central Intercollegiate Athletic Association Tennis Championships. She spent her last two years of college focused on playing against women and later competed in the NCAA Championships. She finished her college career lettering in five sports. In 2009, she was inducted into the Black Tennis Hall of Fame.

Tina Watanabe, a Japanese American from California, was the youngest member of the team. Tina was about twelve years old, and she was petite and pretty and had a classic all-around game. She went on to play the Women's Tennis Association professional tour.

I returned to DC after training with Dr. Johnson and promptly won several USTA tournaments. Most of them were held at country clubs in the DC metropolitan area. Two of them discontinued holding their tournaments after I won them.

One tournament—and one of the most memorable I played during that time—was held at the Belle Haven Country Club in northern Virginia. Belle Haven was then, as it is now, a beautiful club with lush, manicured grounds and excellently maintained courts. On the first day of the tournament, I was told by the tournament director that I could not swim in Belle Haven's pool. I later learned that no such restriction had been placed on the other tournament participants, all of whom were white.

I played Chad Hazam—my good friend and doubles partner—in the tournament final. It was a very hot and humid summer day. We played on a court that was overlooked by a walkway that also surrounded the club's dining room. During the long, hard-fought match, members of the waitstaff, all of whom were black, came outside and peered over the railing to see how I was doing. There were other attendees who clapped at a good shot, but the waitstaff said nothing though it was clear to me they were pulling for me to make a good showing. Following the match, which I won, I went to the locker room and showered. Several of the black waiters came down and gave me knowing nods. To me, it was a silent standing ovation that was most gratifying.

Chad and I have maintained our friendship as we each faced downturns and triumphs over the years. Chad went to the University of Pennsylvania and George Washington University Law School before creating very successful businesses, including owning several Popeye's fast-food franchises, a furniture- and appliance-rental business, and a business that provided cellular phone service to those who could not Otherwise afford it because of bad credit. I was very pleased to have his daughter, Lexi, as my law clerk. She was terrific, working without pay for a week past the time of her clerkship to help me resolve a complicated case that was important in sustaining the Environmental Protection Agency's authority and ability to regulate carbon omissions by the trucking industry.

In my final year at Coolidge, I focused on getting into college. Harvey Freishtat, who had graduated from Coolidge and was then a sophomore at Princeton, told me that I should apply to Princeton. I had not thought of applying to Princeton or any other Ivy League school, but he explained that Princeton was changing and that its president, Robert Goheen, wanted to increase the number of black students on Princeton's campus. He was actively looking for "diamonds in the rough." Because of Harvey's recommendation and my memory of him from Paul—the self-possessed and smart kid who was certain to go places—I ended up applying to Princeton. I also applied to Hamilton College, Ohio Wesleyan, where I was recruited and offered a tennis scholarship, and George Washington. While I was fairly confident that I would get into one of these schools, Mom was not. Without my knowledge, she applied to Hampton Institute, a historically black college, which accepted me as well.

Ironically, the event that triggered my longest period of depression and led to my disability retirement was a speaking engagement that I did at the request of Harvey for his retirement celebration. Harvey had been managing partner of McDermott, Will & Emery in Boston. I was very flattered when he asked me to speak and was pleased to know that the other speakers were William Weld, the former governor of Massachusetts, and a justice on Massachusetts's Supreme Judicial Court. I had no difficulty preparing the first part of my remarks and developing an overall theme, but I developed a block when it came to coming up with closing paragraphs. The thought that the speech would not be of a quality I wanted in order to honor my friend quickly started a downward spiral—so much so that I was barely able to function.

Our daughter Alex, who was staying with Al and me after having graduated from Princeton, called Al who had gone to San Francisco on a business trip to voice her concern because I was crying and apparently having a mental breakdown. A most touching memory I have of Alex is of her holding my hand as I sat in a chair in our kitchen breaking down in front of the TV and telling me that I would be all right and would deliver a great speech.

Randy attended Harvey's retirement celebration because Al asked him to accompany me. She was fearful that I would break down without support. My speech, the last paragraph of which Randy helped me craft, was a roaring success. I spoke about Harvey when he was a student at Paul Junior High, about his habit of wearing starched white shirts and colorful sleeveless vests, about his family not fleeing the neighborhood as other white families had, and about how he encouraged me to apply to Princeton. I ended my speech by saying that Harvey's encouragement changed for the better the trajectory of my life and that I was so pleased to publicly thank him for that. The attendees gave me an extended ovation. Harvey was obviously also very pleased and, having no idea that the speech had plummeted me into an episode of depression, he asked me to reprise the speech at another celebration for him in Florida. I declined.

I received Princeton's acceptance letter the day Coolidge played Mercersburg Academy in Pennsylvania. The tennis team returned home after being soundly defeated. I was in Mr. Himes's big, black Buick. When he pulled in front of my house, my parents and Randy were jumping up and down—and Mom was waving a letter. The letter was Princeton's notification that I had been accepted into the class of 1970. There was unadulterated joy on their faces, seemingly aware—though they could hardly appreciate it at the time—that my going to Princeton would change the trajectory of our lives for the better. We did not know then that because of my good experience at Princeton my brother Randy would go there as would my sister, Angela Acree, both daughters, Morgan and Alexandra, a nephew, David Clark, and a niece, Rachel.

6 CHAPTER
PRINCETON

I began my college years in September 1966. Mom and Dad drove me to Princeton, the first time either of them had been there. I rode in the back seat of our car with Randy and my belongings that did not fit in the trunk. My sister Angela, then three years old, did not accompany us.

When we turned onto Washington Road off of Route 1, a lump came to my throat. I saw the regal spires of the Princeton graduate school in the distance. I thought, *I sure hope I have not bitten off more than I can chew.* That thought persisted until my junior year.

As the son of a mother who had graduated from college and held a master's degree from New York University, a father who had attended three colleges, and born into a family who always saw education as the way to succeed, I always knew I was going to college. I had never supposed, however, that I would attend an Ivy League university, one that had been founded in 1746, twenty years before the Declaration of Independence and had graduated so many notable alumni. Forty -one Nobel laureates, twenty-one National Medal of Science winners, fourteen Fields Medalists, five Abel Prize winners, ten Turing Award laureates, five National Humanities Medal recipients, 209 Rhodes scholars, 139 Gates Cambridge Scholars, 126 Marshall scholars, two US presidents, and twelve US Supreme Court Justices (three of whom currently serve on the court), and numerous living billionaires and foreign heads of state are all counted among Princeton's alumni. Princeton has also graduated many prominent members of the US Congress and the US cabinet, including eight secretaries of state, three secretaries of defense and two of the past four chairs of the Federal Reserve.

Princeton's collegiate gothic architecture is purposely imposing as is the aim of its visual impact. Ralph Adams Cram, arguably the leading Gothic Revival architect and theoretician in the early twentieth century, explained the appeal of the Gothic for educational facilities in his book *Gothic Quest* as follows:

Through architecture and its allied arts we have the power to bend men and sway them as few have who depended on the spoken word. It is for us, as part of our duty as our highest privilege to act ... for spreading what is true.

I was not surprised when my parents did not linger after dropping me off. After helping me carry my belongings up the three flights of concrete stairs to my room on the third floor of Pyne Hall and greeting my roommates, Richard "Rick" Webber and Donald Kendall, and their parents, they wished me well and, without pausing even to eat, returned to DC. In family lore, this became known as my parents' "drive-by." They doubtless felt as intimidated and out of place as I did. Pyne Hall, like many of the other dormitories at Princeton, looked like a cathedral.

Rick is from Excelsior, Minnesota, and attended the exclusive Blake School in Hopkins, Minnesota. Rick was a smart, skinny kid with whom I ended up rooming for three years. Donald Kendall is from Bennington, Vermont, and attended the Berkshire School in Sheffield, Massachusetts. Donald was our roommate for about two weeks but then left to live in a single. It was not until twenty years after our graduation when Rick, who had graduated from the University of Michigan Law School and had become a partner at the Arent Fox law firm in DC, told me over lunch that when my parents and I had left our room to pick up another load of my things from our car, his father turned to him and said, "Don't worry. We can get you another room." Rick was sure that his father's statement was meant to be words of comfort to assure him that he would not have to suffer sharing a dorm room with a black person. Rick was shocked, as his dad had not evidenced any signs of racism before then.

As it turns out, Rick and I got along exceedingly well and roomed together until our senior year. We remain good friends and over the years have shared each other's good fortunes and challenges.

My first weeks at Princeton were filled with anxiety. There were thirteen African Americans in my class of 825. My white classmates (and two African students) had a certain way of carrying themselves that bespoke a confidence that is possessed by many of the scions of wealth and privilege. Their bearing and the inflection of their voices when they expressed themselves about everything from current events to the courses they had signed up to take to the girls they would date said, "I belong here." Their way of talking and walking was intimidating to say the least.

The intimidation I felt was not helped by the traditional freshmen assembly in Alexander Hall during the first week of school when E. Alden Dunham, then Princeton's admissions director, talked to us about our class. It was crystal clear to me that I was an affirmative action admit. My SAT scores were far lower than the scores of the rest of the class. We learned that out of 5,692 applications Princeton admitted 1,265. Though the 40 percent prep school ratio was normal, for the first time in history, fewer than half of the sons of alumni who applied were admitted. We also learned that our class had a great number of senior class presidents, heads of student government, captains of high school football, basketball, and tennis teams, and National Merit Scholars. We also had acclaimed musicians and students doing all kinds of notable things. We were slightly less academically accomplished but considerably more athletic than the class of 1969, a proposition that was proven true when two weeks after Dunham's presentation the class of 1970 walloped the class of 1969 in Cane Spree, a series of athletic events pitting the freshmen against the sophomore class in tennis, swimming, track and field, and other sports contests. The freshman class of 1970 Cane Spree victory was the first since 1958.

I was not the only black student who felt ill at ease. The day after my parents dropped me off, I was walking along Nassau Street, the town's main drag, and saw Robert Middleton, a black student from the District of Columbia whom I had met and last seen at an event for Princeton admits from the Washington metropolitan area. Middleton's mother was the principal of Spingarn High School in DC. Middleton was walking in the opposite direction. When we made eye contact, we ran toward each other like long-lost friends and warmly embraced. It did not have to be said. We both felt comfort at seeing someone who looked like us.

I came to learn that it was not only blacks who felt ill at ease at Princeton. I was a term trustee on Princeton's board of trustees from 2000 to 2004. At the traditional retiring trustees' dinner, where retiring trustees speak about some aspect of their Princeton experience, a very accomplished white journalist employed by the *Washington Post* who had attended a public high school spoke at length and in a heartfelt way about how uncomfortable he felt being one of the relatively few students in the 1950s who had not prepared at one of the elite private schools that typically send their graduates to Princeton and other elite universities.

During my first year at Princeton, almost all of my time except on Sundays was devoted to studying for and attending classes and playing for the freshmen tennis team. I also had employment washing dishes at Commons, where underclassmen took their meals. On Sundays, I often performed duties as a chapel deacon when I ushered in the university chapel.

The amount of time I spent studying in Firestone Library earned me the moniker "spook of the library," a fact Al learned when she and I attended a black alumni party in Washington. She was thoroughly bemused.

I met the dean of the chapel, Ernest Gordon, during my first few weeks at the university. I was impressed with this thoroughly kind man who spoke with conviction about social justice in his heavy Scottish brogue in uplifting sermons. When the Vietnam War raged—as did the protests against it—Gordon gave several anti-war speeches. One of his acts that endeared him to those students who, like me, opposed the war (about 80 percent of us) was to permit the university chapel to be used for students to protest by burning their draft cards, an illegal act that I applauded. I had a lottery number, which I learned from a TV broadcast, that meant I would not be drafted.

Dean Gordon was not one of those know-it-all Christians who had the luxury of being without doubt about anything, including his faith. This humility stemmed from his personal history. Gordon, a native of Scotland, was a war hero. He was a company commander with the Second Battalion, Argyll and Sutherland Highlanders, and fought several battles in the Malayan Campaign and the Battle of Singapore during World War II. After the capture of Singapore, he escaped to Java and attempted to sail several thousand miles from Padang to Sri Lanka with a group of other British officers in a native fishing boat. He was captured and was returned to Singapore as a prisoner of war. During his captivity, Gordon found his sense of self and spirituality when he was brutally forced to help build the Bridge on the River Kwai. The Japanese were especially cruel to their prisoners, leading to an extraordinarily high death rate.

Gordon was subjected to all manner of torture, leading him to be placed in the "death" ward, which was designated for those who were not expected to survive. He was treated there by two special soldiers in their late twenties, a Methodist named Dust Miller, a gardener from New Castle, and Dinty Moore, a devout Roman Catholic. The two gave twenty-four-hour care to Gordon. They boiled rags and cleaned and massaged Gordon's diseased legs every day. To the great surprise of everybody, Gordon survived. As a consequence, many of the POWs experienced a revival of faith and hope for life. Dean Gordon never talked with me about his experiences during the war, but it was clear his experiences were the crucible for forging spiritual and religious faith that were easy to see.

I went to chapel services at Princeton because I was accustomed to attending Sunday services. At one time, I had given thought to studying to become a minister, a thought that I am sure grew from the seed planted by my parents. They both were religious and insisted that each member of our family attend worship services wherever we were living. In Columbia, we attended

Wesley Methodist church and joined Asbury United Methodist Church in 1955 as soon as we moved to DC from South Carolina. The minister at that time was James D. Foy, a man who was a bit overweight and delivered sermons that were dry and not inspiring to an eight-year-old. I was confirmed at Asbury and received my Bible signed by Reverend Foy and the superintendent of the Sunday school, Mary E. Hawkins, on September 29, 1957.

After a Sunday chapel service in the spring of 1967 at the Princeton chapel, I met a woman who was to become a lifelong friend, confidant, and spiritual adviser. Toward the end of the service, I heard the most beautiful voice singing a soaring hymn solo. I asked someone in a position to know who sang the song and asked that he introduce her to me. I was introduced that morning to Gail Fields, a student at the Westminster Choir College, which was located in the town of Princeton.

Gail is an authentically devout Christian. We talked a few minutes that day and again at length at a church-sponsored picnic a few weeks after our first meeting. We did not see each other often in Princeton after that, but following our graduations, we talked frequently after I contacted her to seek her advice regarding my failing marriage to my first wife.

Also, it was to Gail that I lamented about the psychological pain I was experiencing during my depressive episodes. Gail was always willing to listen and often delivered therapeutic tough love. Often when I was feeling sorry for myself she prodded me to appreciate all that I had and always had a story to tell regarding the faith that others had in Jesus Christ that sustained them during hard times and that they exhibited even when it seemed that they had been abandoned by all who mattered—even God himself. She frequently speaks of faith, the importance of never losing hope, and living in accordance with the Word of God as literally set forth in the Bible.

Academically, I struggled to keep up with my fellow students, particularly during my first two years at Princeton. They were extremely bright and, unlike me, were well prepared to meet the academic rigor of Princeton's course offerings. Many of them had attended private schools. Princeton's professors and preceptors were extremely knowledgeable and demanding as well.

In one of my courses my first year, a preceptor's interest in me and in teaching me the skills of expository writing provided the foundation for my excelling in written communication ever since. Professor Albert Sonnenfeld taught Modern European Literature 101, and his lectures were given in McCosh 10. McCosh 10 is a lecture hall in McCosh, a building that from the outside looks like a small Gothic cathedral. The lecture hall is a semicircle with about sixty wooden high-backed seats. European Literature 101, like most Princeton courses, involved a lecture twice a week and then a discussion of the course material in small sections, called precepts, often led by a graduate teaching assistant.

The first assignment for the course was to write a five-page paper that traced the leitmotif in three novels written by European authors: *Death in Venice* by Thomas Mann, *The Metamorphosis* by Franz Kafka, and *Waiting for Godot* by Samuel Beckett. I valiantly struggled with this paper, devoting almost all of my time to writing drafts of it. By contrast, Rick wrote his paper in two nights.

In those days, Princeton had a numerical grading system from 1 to 7, with further refinement of a "+" or "–," with 1+ being the top grade one could achieve. I received a 4– on my paper, the equivalent of a C–. I was very disappointed. I had not indulged the thought that I would get above a 2, but I certainly did not expect a 4–, the lowest grade I had ever received, especially after devoting many hours trying to craft as good a paper as I could. Rick got a 2– on his paper and had not devoted nearly as much time on the assignment as I had.

I went to Stanley Corngold to complain. Corngold, a graduate of Columbia and Cornell, conducted the preceptorial I was assigned for the course. After hearing me out, Corngold looked me in the eye and said, "Mr. Kennedy, you do not know how to write, but if you are willing to put in some extra time, I will teach you."

For the following six months, I had weekly one-on-one meetings with Corngold. He taught me expository writing and how to approach writing assignments like the one I had botched. Unlike high school writing assignments, I was not being asked to simply write book reports. I had to delve beneath the words of the author in order to fully discern what the words were meant to convey and the book's dominant themes. Often the words of a novel are not meant to be a mirror reflection of the author's thinking; they reflect the author's perspective obliquely. I learned how to structure my thoughts and present them clearly.

One of the first students with whom I had a conversation at Princeton was Kirk Unruh. Kirk had gone to the elite Saint Paul School in Baltimore and was a standout lacrosse player. I do not recall the setting, but we were alone and talked about our backgrounds. When Kirk learned that I was from the District of Columbia, he excitedly blurted, "Do you like soul music?" I was taken aback because this was said with apparent sincerity by a youngster who looked and sounded as vanilla as could be. For a moment, I simply did not know how to react. Perhaps because of the intimidation I was feeling, generally leading me to be on guard at all times, I momentarily considered not being truthful and telling him that I did not like soul music at all but rather liked classical music.

Fortunately, I answered truthfully and told Kirk that I did indeed like soul music. For about forty-five minutes, we talked about artists we liked and the songs they had made popular" "Soul Man" by Sam and Dave, "Ooh Baby Baby" by Smokey Robinson and the Miracles, "Mustang Sally" by "the Wicked" Wilson Pickett, "Gypsy Woman" by Curtis Mayfield, and others. We also talked about the venues where these artists performed, some of which we had experienced like the Apollo in New York City, the Lincoln Theater in Washington, and Carr's and Sparrows Beach on the Chesapeake Bay. I learned that Kirk had gone to some venues that I had avoided, given the "roughness" of the audiences that typically were in attendance. I thoroughly enjoyed that conversation with Kirk, and it went a long way in settling me down as I had made a connection with a person who understood the culture that had shaped me.

Kirk and I became good friends, and I soon came to appreciate what a thoroughly fine person he is. He is devoted to family, friends, this country, and Princeton University—where he serves as its director of development relations. It is no surprise that Kirk rose to the rank of rear admiral in the navy and has received many honors for his outstanding performance while serving as deputy commander of the Maritime Defense Zone Atlantic, which plans for the defense of vital sea areas, including ports, harbors, and navigable waters of the United States and overseas in times of war. Among the honors he received is the Legion of Merit medal, one of the military's highest awards.

My friendship with Kirk—like others I began at Princeton, Paul Junior High, and Coolidge High School—greatly influenced my thinking about race relations. One thought that I have is that if everyone in the world could spend just five minutes talking with each other member of our planet, there would not be anywhere near as much racism, racialism, or racial resentment. We would realize that we share common concerns, hopes, and dreams—many of them having to do with what we want for our children—that have nothing to do with the veneer of our skin. Given this attitude, I have not hesitated to interact with people who do not look like me and have been receptive to their friendship as well.

Another white student at Princeton with whom I established a friendship is Richard Howell. I was introduced to Richard by Kirk. I do not remember the occasion, but I vividly remember my reaction the first time I heard the sound of Richard's voice. Richard, whose nickname is Dixie, is from Atlanta. He had—and continues to have—the kind of southern drawl that black folks associate with that of a cotton plantation's overseer. I had not heard such an accent since my family moved from South Carolina.

Howell was one of the most determined tennis, players I have ever met. He played number two on the freshmen team behind Bobby Goeltz.

Howell's family is steeped in tennis tradition and excellence. In 1964, the Howell family was selected as the Tennis Family of the Year by the Southern Tennis Association. His mother, Caroline Howell, was inducted in 2000 as a member of the Georgia Tennis Hall of Fame and was joined by Richard in 1993 and Richard's brother Peter in 2010.

Richard's father and brother "Speed" had gone to Princeton before him. As a player, Richard had little flash, but he was superbly conditioned, smart, and determined. It is not surprising that Richard went on to become a very successful sports agent. In 1993 Richard, a lawyer, became famous for negotiating Emmitt Smith's elephantine multimillion- dollar contract (then the highest ever for a football player) with the Dallas Cowboys. The Cowboys owner, Jerry Jones, and coach, Jimmy Johnson, called Richard "the agent from hell."

My sophomore year, 1967–1968, I roomed with Rick in a dorm room that F. Scott Fitzgerald had lived in. Fitzgerald was the author of *The Great Gatsby*, one of the greatest American novels ever written and the definitive portrait of the roaring twenties—or, as Fitzgerald called it, the Jazz Age. It was a large dorm room with two separate sleeping quarters and a common living room that was burnished with polished dark wood accents and a large fireplace.

F. Scott, like me, suffered from depression and had an intense and, some would say, pathological fear of failure as well.

Me in my freshman year at Princeton in the spring of 1967.

As in my freshman year, I did very little in my sophomore year other than study and play tennis. Unlike my roommate, I never went to the mixers that drew most of the white students. My attitude was that any time I was not devoting myself to a constructive academic or athletic pursuit, I was letting Mom and Dad down and not doing my best. Dad always instructed that "more important than the will to win is the will to prepare to win." Thus, it was unusual when I attended a football game pitting Princeton against Yale at Palmer Stadium in the fall of 1967.

It was a misty day, so I carried an umbrella. On the way to the game, I saw Carl Frankel, a classmate I knew from DC. He was a fellow competitor in local tennis tournaments. Carl was accompanied by a cute girl, Betsy Paull, who was a senior in high school at the Sidwell Friends School, an upscale private school in the District of Columbia that Carl also had attended. Betsy had been invited by Carl to visit for the weekend. I offered to walk with them so that Betsy could be protected from the mist by my umbrella. We ended up sitting together in the stands of Palmer Stadium, and I carried on a lively conversation with the both of them. At some point during our time together, I got the impression that Betsy would welcome a call from me to set up a date when we both were in DC.

For stadium aficionados, Palmer Stadium—a stadium on the campus—hosted the Princeton University football team, as well as its track and field team, from 1914 until 1996, when it was replaced by the Princeton University Stadium. Palmer Stadium was named for Stephen S. Palmer, a trustee of the university, by his son, Edgar Palmer III. From 1936 to its closing, the track's long jump record was held by Jesse Owens.

When I returned to DC for the Thanksgiving holiday, I called Betsy and made a date to see a movie. Her mother, Elsie Paull, suggested *African Queen*. Mrs. Paull had a facial resemblance and demeanor similar to that of Katherine Hepburn, who starred with Humphrey Bogart in the classic movie.

I had a very unsettled feeling in my stomach as I drove to Betsy's house west of Rock Creek Park to pick her up for our date. I had not dated a white girl before and did not know how I would be received by her parents. I was pleasantly surprised when they both greeted me warmly.

That spring, Betsy invited me to escort her to her senior prom. It was an interesting and fun date. I felt very cool wearing a denim work shirt with my classic tuxedo. I developed a meaningful relationship with Betsy, and we dated throughout college and for periods of time after my first marriage and up until the time of hers. I also developed a wonderful relationship with her parents that continued until they died, Mrs. Paul at the age of one hundred and Mr. Paul at the age of ninetysix.

Mrs. Paull was an extraordinary woman. She attended the private Maret School in DC where everything was taught in French—even algebra and Latin. Her mother thought she needed broader experience than could be provided by Maret, so Mrs. Paull and her sister were sent to a public school, Central High School, now Cardozo, where she graduated when she was fifteen. She was too young for college, so she was sent to a boarding school in Lausanne, Switzerland, for a year. Thereafter, she spent time at the Boston Conservatory training to be an opera singer. Soon thereafter, she discarded that dream and enrolled at Barnard College in New York City.

Betsy's mother's first husband, Francis Swann, had been a friend of F. Scott Fitzgerald and, like Fitzgerald, had been in the Princeton class of 1935. Also like Fitzgerald, he was a writer and alcoholic. Mrs. Paull and "Swannie" were married for seven years. Betsy reckoned that part of her mother's affection for me was due to my connection to Princeton and the memories I invoked of her flapper years. They had lived in Hollywood, and Swannie was a screenwriter for film and television and a producer of stage performances. His most well-known work is *Out of the Frying Plan*, which had a significant run on Broadway. The play tells the story of three young men and three young women who share an apartment in New York City. They want to be stage folk. Their apartment is immediately above the apartment of a Broadway producer who comes to their apartment. They aren't going to let him go until he sees some evidence of their ability. They stage a murder that is so realistic that police swarm onto the scene, with hilarious results.

Mr. Paull was very knowledgeable about many things and very intellectually curious. When I met Betsy, he was a lawyer who represented indigent defendants. For many years before that, he had been a newspaper journalist. I believe I made my bones with him during an academic break from Harvard Law School when I crafted a statement of facts for a brief he was preparing in connection with an appeal to the United States Court of Appeals for the District of Columbia Circuit. He complimented me, saying that my work was fully equal to that of a seasoned lawyer. This made me feel good and contributed to my feeling confident that I could succeed at Harvard Law and in the practice of law.

My relationship with Betsy was a very good one. With Betsy, I had a relationship, my first intimate one, with a bright person who was knowledgeable about and concerned with racial justice. She also was affectionate and a romantic. She was more progressive than me in her thinking about race matters and urged me to express my blackness publicly much more than I was inclined to do. Once when we were in Manhattan visiting her aunt, Louise "Lulu" Behrend, a teacher at the famed Julliard School of Music who was responsible for kicking Neil Sedaka out of the school, we passed a young black man who raised his balled fist and aggressively said to me, "Black power," in the manner of young blacks during those times. I nodded in his direction but said and did nothing more. Betsy promptly and pointedly told me that I should have raised my fist and given a black power salute in return, a gesture with which I was uncomfortable. In fact, Betsy was much more drawn to the increasing number of idioms suggestive of black pride than was I. I thought many of them bordered on being silly. The only exception was my appreciation for James Brown's hit song "I'm Black and I'm Proud," an anthem I still love.

In my junior year, Betsy visited on the weekend Princeton played Harvard in Princeton's homecoming game. After the game, we went to Woodrow Wilson College, where many upperclassmen like me who did not join eating clubs took their meals. Because it was homecoming, many parents and alumni were there. When we walked into Wilson College, we saw a group of white students and their parents transfixed by a short dark-skinned black student performing the "signifying monkey," a character in African American folklore featuring a monkey using profane language in making fun of other animals in the jungle. The student was prancing around the reception area clearly enjoying the spectacle he was creating.

The signifying monkey's coarse and insulting narrations reminded me of the "joning" and "counting the dozens" that I'd found so entertaining during my time at Paul Junior High. Now, I was beyond embarrassed. The performer and I were the only black people in a room that obviously had been intended to be a venue for genteel conversation while sipping wine. When I was just about to leave, the performer went to a nearby piano, sat down, and began playing beautiful classical music. His audience was just as transfixed by his piano playing as it was with his signifying monkey performance, perhaps more so.

The performing student was David Evans, a graduate student who was pursuing a degree in mechanical engineering. David has a most interesting background. The son of two Arkansas sharecroppers who had six years of education between them, Evans was orphaned by the age of sixteen. However, his parents' untimely deaths did not prevent them from inspiring their seven children with a message that would send them on paths to great success.

David attended Tennessee State University before studying engineering at Princeton. He went on to become the senior admissions officer for Harvard University, where, to date, he has helped select thirty-seven Harvard classes. He has been honored by Harvard several times both for his admissions work and for his activism on behalf of minority groups on and off campus. His portrait hangs in Harvard's Fogg Museum. He is a prolific writer, and his editorials addressing current events and their counterparts in history are published frequently in the *New York Times* and the *Boston Globe*.

My senior year, Betsy studied in Paris. We wrote letters to each other frequently in which we explained what we were doing in precise prose, but we mostly conveyed our affection for each other in surprisingly elegant and nuanced terms.

I devoted a great deal of my time to the tennis team in my senior year. The team was very strong, the number one team in the East. I practiced hard, but I never was able to rise above number seven or eight on the depth chart. This meant that sometimes in competition I did not play, and when I was selected to play, it was always to play doubles. Our number one player was Bobby Goeltz, who had gone to Landon and had won the National Interscholastic championships three years in a row. The only other player to have accomplished this feat was Arthur Ashe.

My senior year, Goeltz finished the season with an 8–2 singles record. Goeltz was a tremendous talent, but he sometimes was unfocused and quirky. At Princeton, as he had done in DC when he played me, Goeltz would leave his shoelaces untied while competing. Richard Howell played number two and turned in a 9–1 season in singles. Richard, while not nearly as natural talented as Goeltz, was a gritty player with an iron will to win. In the third spot was captain Will Irwin, who went undefeated in 1969–1970. Scott Rogers played number four, going 10–3, and Rick Weir played number five and went 8–5. Andy Krusen had a 7–3 season. Krusen, an extraordinarily handsome student from Florida, provided something to talk about, as he dated a girl who was heir to the Hanes underwear fortune. She often came to watch Andy play.

I loved tennis practice and playing on the courts in the middle of campus where Whitman College now sits. A distinctive pagoda separated the two banks of clay courts, which were overlooked by a grassy knoll where spectators sat and watched our matches and sometimes even our practices. A plaque on the pagoda bore stanzas from "If" by Rudyard Kipling, my favorite poem. The poem provides an excellent tutorial on how best to live life.

Surprisingly, it was in connection with tennis that I believe my race mattered at Princeton. In my junior year, I was playing well and thought I could beat some of the players who had been placed higher than me on the team depth chart by our coach, John Conroy, and thus designated to play singles. After all, only about two years earlier, I had lost to Bobby

Goeltz, Princeton's number one player, in a very tight 7–5, 7–5 match. Also, only three years earlier, I had defeated Harold Solomon, who was playing number one at Rice University and certainly could beat any of the players on our team. Moreover, I had practiced with several of the singles players and had a basis for assessing their games and how theirs stacked up against mine.

I approached Coach Conroy and inquired about how I might compete to play singles since, to that point, sometimes he did not designate me to play league matches at all or only to play doubles. Conroy, with whom I had always had cordial relations and who often joked around with me, calling me "Henri" and using a put-on French accent, became visibly annoyed and told me emphatically, "You will never play for Princeton." Conroy did not explain what he meant, and in the absence of further explanation as to his position, I felt that my race had something to do with his negative declaration.

The freshmen tennis team

I did nothing in response to Conroy's reaction. Indeed, I never considered doing so for three reasons. First, I was well aware that Conroy had been the well-regarded tennis coach at Princeton for many years. He had been doing things his way long before I came along. Therefore, his success shielded him from any complaints about how he did things. Second, who would be the person to whom I would protest? And more important than anything else, a protest of any consequence would require me to devote time and energy that would be better utilized doing what I had come to Princeton to do: study and get the best education I could.

While my waking hours were devoted almost entirely to tennis and studying, I did attend a few of the meetings and activities sponsored by Princeton's black student organization, the Association of Black Collegians, including one of the first meetings during which a name was selected for the organization. My suggestion, "The Association of Negro Students," was met with cold silence. The name initially selected, "Association of Black Collegiates," was discarded at the next meeting because someone determined that "Collegiates" was grammatically incorrect. The name eventually selected, "Association of Black Collegians," found favor with many of our members because of the stylish sequence of the initialism ABC.

ABC sponsored a few social events, including a party to which women from area Catholic colleges were invited. When the student organizing this event announced this at an ABC meeting, saying some sisters had been invited from these colleges, a wag asked, "Are these sisters, sister sisters, white sisters, or all three?" Truly amusing!

Another ABC-sponsored event involved about eight of us visiting Vassar College in Poughkeepsie, New York, where we were to be introduced to some female African American students. When we arrived and were ushered into one of Vassar's impressively ornate dorm facilities, a matronly white woman told us of the evening's agenda. It was a throwback to much earlier times when young men were introduced to women and would be entertained with them at a "tea."

The young women were introduced separately by the woman as they descended an ornate carpeted staircase. When a particularly attractive student whose nickname was Sam, for Samantha, came down the staircase, Gerald Horne blurted out, "Well, if that is Sam, I want to see Joe and Willie too." The matronly woman was none too pleased at the laugh this got.

Gerald Horne is now a college professor and a prolific Marxist author and historian. He has published on W. E. B. Du Bois and has written books on a wide range of neglected but by no means marginal or minor episodes of world history. He writes about topics he perceives as misrepresented struggles for justice, in particular communist struggles and struggles against imperialism, colonialism, fascism, and racism.

My years at Princeton were marked by student protests over issues associated with the war in Vietnam, the presence of ROTC on campus, and Princeton's investments in companies that profited from their operations in apartheid South Africa. I participated in two protests.

During my freshman year, 1966–1967, George Wallace, the former governor of Alabama, was invited to speak on campus at Dillon Gymnasium. Two years before, in his inaugural address after winning election as Alabama's governor, he thundered, "Segregation now, segregation tomorrow, segregation forever," and stood in the entrance to the University of Alabama in an attempt to stop the enrollment of black students. The members of ABC debated how to protest Wallace's presence. Several members thought we should heckle, shout him down, and prevent him from speaking.

Instead, we arrived early for his presentation dressed in coats and ties and sat together in the first two rows of the audience. When Wallace stood up to speak to the jam-packed audience, we stood as one, and without saying a word, we walked out of the gym, backs straight, displaying dignity and an appreciation for the right of others to hear what Wallace had to say. We received a standing ovation from our fellow students. I could not have been prouder of our protest.

Another protest was one of many on college campuses around the country by those who thought, correctly it turned out, that the system of racial segregation in South Africa could be brought to its knees were the government there required to deal with the economic hardship apartheid brought about. Such hardship would happen if corporations were to withdraw from that country, something that businesses would surely do were they to lose market share and large institutional investors like Princeton.

I was a reluctant participant in this protest. The protest called for members of ABC to take over New South, a large multistory administrative building containing offices, and not permit those employed there to enter. I was reluctant because the protest involved breaking the law and would consume more time than I normally devoted to anything but studying. I joined the protest, however, principally because of the encouragement of Brent Henry in the class of 1969, one of the most impressive students, black or white, I had met at Princeton. Brent was smart, handsome, and stylish with his wire-rim glasses and short-cropped "Fro." He was so cool, which accounted for his nickname, Breeze, short for "Cool Breeze." This nickname was perfect for Brent as it described his demeanor, at all times calm and collected, and his ability to advocate a position using just the right words to set forth indisputable logic. It is no surprise then that, years later, Brent became a term and charter trustee of Princeton and vice chair of the trustee's executive committee. Brent was called upon to investigate some of the most sensitive controversies confronting Princeton. Brent graduated from Yale Law School and now is a partner at Mintz, a leading law firm, which he joined after serving as vice president and general counsel of Partners HealthCare System, an integrated teaching, research, and health care delivery network based in Boston.

To execute our takeover, we formed "cells" and descended upon New South as soon as it was opened by security personnel. We then chain-locked the entrances to the building and prevented anyone but ABC members, including the members of the Princeton chapter of Students for a Democratic Society (SDS) who wanted to support us, from entering. Roderick Hamilton, the president of ABC in the class of 1969, then presented our demands to the university and the press in a carefully worded statement. It was our demand that Princeton disengage from companies that did business in South Africa.

My thoughts about participating in the takeover of New South turned to terror when about six hours after our takeover we heard press reports on the radio that the university had authorized New Jersey state troopers to clear the building and end the protest. The thought of how my father and mother would react to my being suspended or expelled for my part in the protest was terrifying. While I was always impressed by Rod Hamilton, particularly the way he presided over ABC meetings, I came to appreciate him even more when he found a face-saving way to leave New South without confronting state law enforcement officers. Rod penned and delivered a statement that went something like this: "Now that the University has diverted its attention from the subject of our protest to the way we have made that protest, we shall leave this place confident that the university has heard us and appreciate the rightness of our position." After Rod read this statement, we left New South before the troopers arrived, but not before I did my part in contributing to the way the protest would be favorably reported by the press and regarded by our fellow students and university administrators.

When we were about to leave New South, I noticed a couple of students with boxes of steaks under their arms that obviously had been taken from New South's cafeteria. When I challenged them, they attempted to justify their theft by articulating the "we--an oppressed minority-- have the right to 'liberate' the man's property" as recompense, nonsense that had found favor in certain circles that was used to justify looting after the 1960s race riots. I stuck to my guns and persuaded them to return the food to the kitchen. I also made sure the kitchen and the other places we had been were left as we'd found them. I felt good by doing what I felt was the right thing in preventing actions that surely would have subjected our protest to deserved criticism and detracted from our cause.

My experience with these protests colored my views regarding recent efforts by some Princeton students to have Princeton withdraw it memorials to Woodrow Wilson by, among other things, having the Woodrow Wilson School for Public and International Affairs renamed.

My reaction to the Black Justice League's protest is expressed by a criticism that competitive tennis players sometimes level after a particularly poor shot, that shot was "a bad idea poorly executed." The Black Justice League's protest was a bad idea because Wilson, while a racist, as were the vast majority of white men of his time, was not memorialized by Princeton because of his views regarding race but because of the many notable and undeniably good deeds he performed over his lifetime. These included, as president of the United States, supporting passage of progressive legislative policies unparalleled until the New Deal in 1933. The Federal Reserve Act, Federal Trade Commission Act, the Clayton Antitrust Act, and the Federal Farm Loan Act were but some of these extremely beneficent policies. His ideology of internationalism was an activist foreign policy calling on the nation to promote global democracy. For his sponsorship of the League of Nations, Wilson was awarded the 1919 Nobel Peace Prize. While president of Princeton, he increased the faculty dramatically—from 112 to 174. The curriculum guidelines he developed proved to be important progressive innovations in the field of higher education. Wilson also appointed the first Jew and the first Roman Catholic to the faculty. To emphasize the development of expertise, Wilson instituted academic departments and a system of core requirements. He raised admission standards at Princeton and replaced the "gentleman's C" with serious study.

The Black Justice League's protest was equally poor, if not more so, in its execution. What reasoning lead the League to conclude that an appropriate feature of their protest should be to take over the offices of Princeton's president? This behavior was a remarkable display of bad manners, something members of the League should have learned to avoid long before coming to Princeton.

Further, the League's response to the report rendered by a special trustee committee tasked with investigating its position was especially juvenile. The committee chaired by Brent Henry determined that, while Wilson should not be dememorialized, Princeton should take pains to accurately and fully reveal the full spectrum of Wilson's life and beliefs, including his actions and inactions born of his racism. Rather than taking a partial win, the League insulted Princeton and Henry by saying that the investigation and report was nothing but an anticipated whitewash.

These students, none of whom I suspect took the time to learn anything about Henry, were disrespectful to him and Princeton and were wrong.

I know of what I speak because I had the great honor and privilege to serve on Princeton's board of trustees from 2000 until 2004. This service gave me an opportunity to witness how Princeton deals with controversial matters such as the dememorialization issue. It simply cannot be said that these issues are prejudged or swept under the rug. Rather, every attempt is made to determine and understand the facts surrounding the issue and then to bring to bear the intellectual rigor and honesty that a great university should devote to important matters.

During my sophomore year, I experienced a most satisfying nonacademic or non-tennis-related event while at Princeton. Muhammed Ali came to campus as part of his speaking tour of colleges and universities. This money-making tour followed his conviction in 1966 for draft evasion for refusing to be conscripted into the US military because of his religious beliefs and opposition to American involvement in the Vietnam War. This was two years after Ali won the heavyweight title.

Ali was scheduled to give two speeches at Princeton. Because the first speech conflicted with a class, I did not attend Ali's first speech but I rushed over to Whig-Clio, Princeton's debating society, which is the oldest college debating club in the country, to get a glimpse of him. I arrived just when Ali was descending the steps of one of the two majestic buildings that housed the debating society. When he reached the bottom step, I dashed by his entourage and blurted out, "Mr. Ali, I respect you so much. You are my hero." I stuck out my hand to shake his. Ali grasped my hand and my arm up to my elbow with his massive hand and said that he appreciated my compliment.

I followed him to Alexander Hall where he gave his second speech. This was the same venue where the dean of admissions told our class how great we were and where it was confirmed to me that I was an outlier. Ali gave a most intelligent speech in which he explained why he had refused to be conscripted and was opposed to the war in Vietnam. He also seemed to speak directly to me and the few black students in attendance about black pride. In his inimical way, he peppered his speech with freestyle rhymes and ended his speech by saying, "Everybody knows that the blacker the berry, the sweeter the juice." He received thunderous applause and left me feeling uplifted.

That speech and a lecture given by Martin Duberman, a professor of American history, were sorely needed balms for my discomfort born of an inferiority complex, one I had tried to hide for years. In one of his lectures Duberman discussed great sub-Saharan African societies and their important contributions to the world, contributions of which I had not heretofore known. He spoke particularly about Timbuktu. In its golden age, the town's numerous black Islamic scholars and extensive trading network made possible an important book trade. Together with the campuses of the Sankor Madasah, an Islamic university, Timbuktu was a scholarly center in Africa. Having seen and read only about poverty and dysfunction on the continent with which I was genetically linked, this information filled a gaping hole in my knowledge about my forbearers.

I majored in the Woodrow Wilson School of Public and International Affairs. In order to major in the Woodrow Wilson School, unlike any other major at Princeton, a student had to apply and be selected. Successfully dealing with the Woodrow Wilson School's rigorous interdisciplinary requirements—courses in politics, history, economics, and sociology—did much for my confidence. In addition to the course requirements, I was required to study a public policy issue and defend whatever position I took before other members of a policy conference both in writing and orally by answering questions in the bowl of the Woodrow Wilson School auditorium, a venue that resembled the main conference auditorium in the United Nations. During my oral defense, questions were posed by members of the conference, Woodrow Wilson School professors—many of whom had served in high-level positions in government—and students who were expected to be fully knowledgeable about all aspects of the policy at issue.

My first project was a study of the issues surrounding the urban renewal controversy stemming from New Jersey's decision to move the New Jersey College of Medicine and Dentistry to the inner city of Newark. This project displaced hundreds of people, most of them black, and caused heated protests over "urban renewal." One of the leaders of the protest was a thin, dark-skinned black man who vowed to shoot anybody who came to the community and spoke or acted in favor of the project. I managed to get an interview with this activist who insisted that we meet in a public space where I was forced to sit with my back to the door and face a gun pointed in my direction on the table in front of him.

The Woodrow Wilson School also provided an internship at *Time Magazine* in New York City. Twice a week, I would take a bus from Princeton to Grand Central Station and then the subway to the Time-Life Building where I would work on light stories for the magazine. One of the most interesting was confirming the rather open rumor that the then-prime minister of Canada, Pierre Trudeau, was dating Barbara Streisand, and would do so in New York City when attending a conference of world leaders in Manhattan.

At the end of my junior year, I was asked by Gary Hoachlander, a white student from Hagerstown, Maryland, who, like me, had taken his meals at Wilson College, an alternative to the eating clubs, to join him and three or four other upperclassmen in creating and operating a community action program. Gary had obtained funding from the Ford Foundation and was interested in establishing a program off campus, the first time this would have been done at Princeton. Although I had a very good experience rooming with Rick Webber my first three years, I told Gary that I would do it. Therefore, for my last year at Princeton, I lived in a house on Witherspoon Street in the middle of Princeton's African American community with Gary Hoachlander, Len Brown, another black student from Arizona, Michael Gage, John Vail, and John Mavros.

The students participating in the community action program had varied backgrounds. John Mavros was born John Mavrogianis. He was of Greek extraction, but when I met him, he had adopted the culture of black people in the way he talked and dressed and in his interests. Mavros's makeover was so thorough that I doubt that many students had any clue that he was "white."

We operated several programs at Community House that were designed to benefit the African American community in Princeton. It was a large frame house located in the small black community four blocks from Princeton's campus. One of the programs I headed was designed to expose neighborhood kids to uplifting and informative films that I obtained from a publishing company within a twenty-minute drive from the house, a trip I made weekly on Fridays in my Volkswagen Beetle that I had with me at Princeton since my sophomore year. I would then show the films on Friday nights. The kids loved them.

One of those kids was the son of a woman who lived next door to Community House. The two connected residences were strangely constructed. There was an upstairs corridor between the second floor of each residence with a window to the corridor from each that permitted one to enter our neighbor's residence through a window from the common corridor and vice versa. I became friends with this neighbor, a middle-aged black woman, who was the mistress of a member of a New Jersey organized crime family. Looking like a caricature of an Italian mobster, the man had slicked-back jet-black hair, wore stylish suits, and would come to visit her on the weekends driving a sleek, shiny black Cadillac with tinted windows.

At first, I thought my neighbor was interested in me only because of the after-school work I was doing with her son. This notion was fairly quickly dispelled, however, when she explicitly made it known that she wished to have a sexual relationship. For several months, we did. Our assignations were always in her home, which I always entered by climbing through the corridor window. We both were aroused by the risk we were taking in being found out by the mobster boyfriend. He never did.

One of the neighbor's attractive girlfriends also took a liking to me. Once when the three of us went out to dinner, I sat next to the girlfriend and across from my neighbor. The three of us were having pleasant conversation when suddenly the friend reached under the table and began caressing my thigh and eventually my genitals. Not knowing what to say and enjoying her touch immensely, I said nothing and focused on keeping my composure so as not to reveal to my neighbor what was going on.

Every Friday night at Community House, we would invite Princeton students to come for dinner and a dance party. At some of these parties, we would only play songs that had versions sung by white and black artists. We played the songs back to back. One Friday night when we had a dinner and party and it was getting late, I announced that I was headed to my room. A girl who attended Douglas, the sister school to Rutgers University, whom I had never seen before that night, followed me upstairs to my bedroom. When I closed the door, immediately and without a word, she shed her clothes, took my hand, and led me to my bed.

A few days later, she told me that she thought she might be pregnant. This news was terrifying. I was about to graduate and envisioned what my parents would say and do upon hearing that I was an expectant father. Aside from what this news meant for my future, it would be clear that I had disregarded the one lesson regarding sex I had received from my father. When I was about sixteen years old and was leaving to go out on a date, Dad told me, "Don't go swimming without an overcoat."

When I told my neighbor about what the Douglas girl told me, she took me into her arms, told me the girl was testing me—and determining whether I might be trapped—and that after a pregnancy test she probably would tell me that she was not pregnant after all. That is exactly what happened.

Most of my time my senior year was devoted to completing my senior thesis. A defining feature of an undergraduate education at Princeton is the requirement that each student complete a senior thesis or a substantial independent research project. I wrote my thesis on "Black Politics in Indiana 1888-1900," a period that had not been studied by scholars because it was assumed that black politics during this period and in the northern states did not exist or was so insignificant as to not warrant study. In my thesis, I documented the politics and political thoughts of the black population in Indiana, a state that had shown as much racial animus toward blacks, if not more, than any other state in the union. It was one of the swing states in presidential elections, and blacks were despised to such an extent that, in 1866, the white population tried to prevent blacks from coming into the state at all. An article incorporated into the state constitution provided that "no Negro or mulatto shall come into or settle in the state, after the adoption of this Constitution." It also provided that persons who employed such Negroes or encouraged them to stay in the state were subject to fines up to $500. Money from such fines was to be used to colonize blacks already in the state.

My thesis adviser was James McPherson, who is widely recognized as this country's leading authority on the history of the Civil War era. McPherson was the president of the American Historical Association in 2003 and was author of *Battle Cry of Freedom,* which earned him the 1989 Pulitzer Prize. It was a delight being guided by this renowned historian and master teacher. He was patient and kind and had numerous suggestions regarding the sources that were available to me. He made me aware of several black historians with whom I should consult, including the great Howard University historian Rayford Logan. I talked with McPherson several times while writing the thesis to make sure I was following the outline we had agreed upon when I started writing and focused on the major issues confronting blacks of that era.

Writing my thesis required that I learn about politics and history at the micro level and perform research in original sources. Much of my research involved reading newspapers that went out of print long ago that I was able to obtain through Princeton's interlibrary loan service, a service I was intimately familiar with as I had worked in that division of the library during my junior year. It also required that I become knowledgeable about persons about whom, like most Americans, I was totally ignorant.

The most fascinating such person was T. Thomas Fortune, an ex-slave who from 1885 until his death in 1928 was a journalist of power and nerve. I read many articles and editorials written by Fortune, who unfortunately remains largely unknown because he left behind no important books or followers and much of his energy was consumed by surviving his mental illness, destitution, and a flawed marriage. He also refused to adopt the role that many whites then loved to assign: "spokesman for his race."

Leaving the Deep South when he was eighteen years old, Fortune's first job was in the print shop of the *People's Advocate*, a Washington weekly. A Howard University student, Fortune began a column where he thundered about political issues and political figures. The job paid little, however, and he soon left for New York City and another paper. In the 1880s, Negro weeklies—always four pages—had small circulations, small staffs, and small chances for survival. One exception was, if only on the last count, was the *Globe*, and Fortune wrote for it. Opinions interested him more than events, so he became an editorial writer. Fortune could rankle people not only on one side of an issue but on both sides. When Frederick

Douglas married a white woman, Fortune criticized those Negroes who opposed interracial marriage. Negroes, he wrote, "are always prating about the unreasonable prejudices of other people and yet show, when occasion presents itself prejudices just as narrow and unreasonable." As for whites, "we are surprised at the amount of gush which intermarriage inspires in this country. It is in strict keeping with all the sophistries kept alive by the papers and the people about the colored people."

Fortune took on both Democrats and Republicans. He denounced Democrats as "the party of stupidity" that "learns nothing and forgets nothing" and denounced Republicans as a "mean, cunning, treacherous organization." Throughout his life, Fortune had no money and little job security, and he lived with constant mental and physical pain—plus racism. Toward the end of his life, in 1927, he was called the "the beloved dean of Negro Journalism" by the National Negro Press Association. On his death, *The Amsterdam News* called Fortune "a young old man, a new Negro, who loved America, while recognizing much in it to hate."

After turning in my thesis on April 15, 1970, I worked hard to earn the highest grades I could, quietly hoping to earn cum laude recognition. I did not graduate cum laude, but I am happy to say that I did not graduate "thank you laude" either. The graduation ceremonies were wonderful, although it was sweltering hot in New Jersey in June of 1970 when there was a once-in-every-seven-years infestation of locusts, also called cicadas. The locusts were so dense that when the graduates marched in front of Nassau Hall we could hear the crunch of their shells breaking underfoot.

I had intended to wear a dashiki during the graduation exercises, but Randy persuaded me not to do so since it would doubtless seem odd in the eyes of my parents and to them entirely inappropriate for the occasion. I am glad I followed Randy's advice. I realized in the following years that the graduation ceremony represented for my parents the realization of one of their defining goals, one that should not in the least be negatively affected by what I wore when I received my degree.

A highlight for me of the graduation exercises was witnessing Bob Dylan being given an honorary degree. Bob Dylan was popular with most of the graduating seniors, but he was even more popular with many black students given Dylan's longtime support for civil rights. The famed singer memorialized the day he received Princeton's honorary degree in his song "The Day of the Locust," a reference to the cicada infestation.

The locust came to be the symbol of our class so that at every reunion or class event thereafter, a bug theme is incorporated in one way or the other. For example, our twenty-fifth reunion year jacket is emblazoned with the Princeton crest with the image of a locust in the middle. Our thirtieth reunion was dubbed the "Return of the Weevil Empire." Corny to be sure, but for me, and I suspect for most members of the class of 1970, this reference to an important day in our lives continues to be an endearing reminder of our good fortune that we will forever be tied together and to Princeton.

For me, the symbol of my association with the members of Princeton's "great class of 1970" is enervating. On a hot and humid day in the late spring of 2016, I was playing in a Category II National tournament at Oglebay Park in Wheeling, West Virginia. My determined opponent had won the first set in two hours. I was tired and starting to falter when a cicada—an insect that is not a very good flier—landed on my shirt. I immediately thought of my graduation day from Princeton, my class's embrace of the cicada as our symbol, and thought, *Win this one for the class—yes, that great class of '70*. My resolve returned, and I got a boost from the memory. I won in three hard-fought, gutsy sets after four hours of play.

7 CHAPTER
HARVARD LAW SCHOOL

I began to think about going to law school after, for one reason or the other, I discerned that my talents would not enable me to succeed in other endeavors I had considered for my life's work. What I might do for my life work was always a most important concern. Before, and certainly after my time at Princeton, I took to heart Princeton's informal motto, which references its aspiration for its graduates "Princeton in the nation's service," which has been expanded to "Princeton in the nation's service and in the service of humanity." Another expression of this sentiment was penned by George Washington Carver: "No individual has any right to come into the world and go out of it without leaving behind him distinct and legitimate reasons for having passed through it."

My interest in the ministry waned soon after I entered Princeton, owing to an overall questioning of my own faith. I had real problems, for example, with Christian doctrine that did not explain how there could be an all-knowing, all-powerful, and beneficent God that would permit innocent suffering. Too, there was no satisfactory explanation for the Christian teaching that heaven is reserved for only those who believe in the divinity of Jesus Christ and thus is denied to most human beings, including those who believe in Islam, Judaism, Buddhism, the only faiths they are taught or to which they are exposed.

My interest in becoming an economist received a slap in the face at the hands of R. Walter Lewis, the 1979 Nobel Prize winner in economics, from whom I took a course entitled "The Economics of Underdeveloped Countries." I took this course after doing relatively well in introductory macro and microeconomic courses I took from Professor Burton Malkiel. I received a 3– in Lewis's course, the equivalent of a B–. It also was in Lewis's course that I was falsely accused by a preceptor, a graduate student teaching assistant, of plagiarism and had great difficulty with regression analysis, a tool for microeconomic analysis.

My interest in becoming a physician faltered when I took biology and had difficulty understanding the principles and science surrounding deoxyribonucleic acid (DNA). I was in a fog during the lectures in the course that attempted to explain how a molecule carries the genetic instructions governing the growth, development, functioning, and reproduction of all known living organisms and many viruses.

I doubtless too was influenced by several of my classmates in the Woodrow Wilson School who were considering law school. I was influenced even more so by my father who talked admiringly of lawyers, particularly of Thurgood Marshall, whom he had seen in action in court in South Carolina when Marshall was arguing cases for the NAACP Legal Defense Fund. At the dinner table, Dad frequently would talk about how commanding a presence Marshall was and how he was accorded respect seldom given to a black man. I also observed that social justice for blacks was advancing much faster through the courts than by other means, where smart lawyers were using the law to advance the cause of black empowerment. Finally, I liked the idea that I could learn skills and work in a profession where I could be my own boss.

Having determined that I wanted to go to law school, I quickly decided that I wanted to go to one of the elite national law schools. Harvard was my first choice. I did well enough on the Law School Aptitude Test, but not so well that I was assured of being accepted there. When I talked with Rod Hamilton from the class of '69 about wanting to go to Harvard, he advised me to get in touch with Walter Leonard, the school's African American assistant dean and assistant director of admissions.

I traveled to Harvard to talk with Dean Leonard regarding my application. This scenario, an African American student talking with Leonard about gaining admission to Harvard Law School, repeated itself many times. Thus, Leonard played a part in the admission of the remarkably talented cadre of black lawyers who entered Harvard Law School in the sixties and seventies. This group of which I am enormously proud among others includes Ted Wells, the super lawyer partner at Paul Weiss who represented the tobacco industry and Citibank in litigation in which millions if not billions of dollars were at stake, George Haywood, an immensely successful private investor, an early financial supporter of Barack Obama, and world record holder for his age division in the 300 high hurdles, Ken Frazier, the CEO of Merck and the first businessman to resign his position on an advisory council after Donald Trump failed to distinguish between the attempt to intimidate by the Ku Klux Klan and neo-Nazis at the University of Virginia, Sylvester Turner, the mayor of Houston who masterfully led the city in confronting the ravages of Hurricane Harvey, and Ken Chenault, the CEO of American Express.

In 1971, after Derek Bok became president of Harvard, he appointed Leonard as a special assistant. In that role, Leonard was the primary force behind the Harvard Plan, a blueprint for establishing equal educational and employment opportunities in higher education. The Harvard Plan was cited approvingly by the United States Supreme Court in *the Regents of the University of California v. Bakke* decision and adopted by hundreds of colleges and universities throughout the country.

My time at Harvard was extremely gratifying for several reasons. Having graduated from Princeton, I was very confident that I could successfully tackle Harvard Law. Because of this confidence, I was not at all intimidated by my fellow students or Harvard as an institution as I had been at Princeton when I began there. For this reason, I did not hesitate to take the most challenging courses and engage my professors. As significant, however, to my overall enjoyment of my Harvard Law years was reconnecting with Bobby O'Meally, my childhood friend, who was pursuing a PhD in English Literature at Harvard's graduate school.

Our first year, we lived together in Perkins Hall, a graduate school dorm. Our accommodations at Perkins consisted of a large living room with a fireplace and a room that was intended to be a bedroom for two occupants. We decided, however, to have Bob in the living room and me in the room intended to be a bedroom. This arrangement proved to be very interesting. For example, because there was only one door to and from our suite in the living room, I had to enter and leave by that door, which required me to pass by Bobby's bed. I always walked softly and averted my eyes as Bobby often had girlfriends who slept over with him. Many of them, as we say back home, were "fine as wine."

During that first year, I came to appreciate just what a romantic my friend had become. I attended the party in Boston where he met Jackie Malone, who was to become his wife. He fell hard for her, and within a week, he had taken her to Walden Pond, a lake in Concord, Massachusetts, known for its association with the writer Henry David Thoreau. He courted her by penning romantic poems, which he would often do when he was in the presence of a pretty woman even if that woman was writhing around a pole in a strip joint and looking forward to earning money giving lap dances.

Bobby and I daily had lively conversations on a variety of subjects, including the use of language. In addition to discussing the contrasting ways in which language is employed in the disciplines we were studying, we had an ongoing debate regarding the value of Ebonics, the language used by many uneducated or undereducated blacks predominantly in the urban centers of our northern cities. I was of the view that there was nothing to recommend its use in formal or even informal conversation. To the contrary, in my view,this patois was an easily recognized badge of the lowest socioeconomic class of African Americans. Bob disagreed and was of the view that Ebonics often was a superior way of describing conduct than formal english. For example, when a narrator describes a walk to the store, is it better to say "I walk to the store" or "I be walking to the store"? Bob's view was that the latter formulation more vividly describes the action of the narrator, giving it a movement the former formulation does not. Recently at a tennis tournament in Sarasota Florida, a fellow African American competitor from Chicago, Bobby Hampton, voiced his agreement with Bob. According to Hampton, Ebonics offered a superior formulation to conventional language in conveying that a person has left. Thus, better than saying that "he left" is to use the Ebonic formulation of "he gone." Likewise, better than representing that the person left some time ago is to say "He be gone." And, to convey that the person left a long time ago, the better narration is "he done been gone." I remain unconvinced.

My favorite first-year law professors were Charles Dawson, who taught contracts, Abram Chayes, who taught civil procedure, and Lloyd Weinreb, who taught criminal law and procedure. These professors were extremely good teachers and went out of their way to make sure students learned how to analyze legal problems—and to "think like a lawyer."

My second year at Harvard Law, I took Constitutional Law, a course taught by Archibald Cox, a legal scholar of the first order noted for his Boston patrician bearing and bow ties. There were two black students in the class, Robert Malson and me. After a stint in the navy, Malson had graduated from Howard University, where he had been a student activist. I was having trouble understanding how the Bill of Rights differed from tort law in governing behavior. Professor Cox explained that the Constitution's Bill of Rights was a prohibition against governmental conduct and that it was tort law that regulated conduct between individuals. To make his point, Cox said that if he were to have a party and did not want to invite me or Malson to it because we were black, the Bill of Rights did not prohibit him from doing so. Obviously, concerned with how this explanation registered with the class, and particularly me and Malson, Professor Cox quickly said that of course were he to have a party to which students were invited Malson and I would be included. I was favorably impressed by Cox's concern and sensitivity regarding race matters.

The morning after his lecture, I bumped into Cox in line ordering breakfast at Harkness Commons, Harvard Law's dining facility. We had breakfast together and did so several times thereafter, each time munching on scrambled eggs doused in catsup the way Cox and I loved them.

Archibald Cox was at the center of events leading to Richard Nixon's resignation in anticipation of his impeachment in 1974, the year following my graduation. History records that Archibald Cox, having been appointed special prosecutor in 1972, successfully subpoenaed the tapes of conversations that had taken place in the Oval Office of the president in connection with Cox's investigation of the Watergate scandal. It is an ironic historical fact that Cox's maternal great-grandfather, William Evarts, was a member of the team that defended President Andrew Johnson, a Democrat who ran with Lincoln on the National Union ticket. In Johnson's impeachment trial before the Senate, Evarts, a devoted Republican, faced down what seemed to be the unstoppable determination of the Republicans to oust the Democrat and accidental president succeeding Abraham Lincoln upon Lincoln's assassination.

In between my second and third year in law school, I worked as a summer associate with the law firm of Jones, Day, Reavis, and Pogue in DC. Jones Day is a very large firm with several offices around the United States with its main office in Cleveland, Ohio. Jones Day, then as now, had a broad corporate practice. During the course of the summer, I worked with several first-rate attorneys, including Erwin Griswold, who had joined Jones Day after an illustrious career. Griswald had been solicitor general of the United States under Lyndon Johnson and Richard Nixon and served twenty years as dean of the Harvard Law School.

I had more contact with the affable Eldon "Took" Crowell. I worked on a few assignments in Crowell's practice area, government contracting, and we talked a fair amount about Princeton and how it differed from his days there to mine. Seven years later, Took would split with Jones Day and start the hugely successful law firm of Crowell and Moring.

I had even more contact with Sturgis Warner. Warner, stricken with polio while a boy, was a remarkably courageous man. Warner reported to work every day, at first walking bent over with a cane and then, toward the end of the summer, in a wheelchair. Warner had helped draft the Twenty-Third Amendment to the Constitution, which was ratified in 1961 and gave Washington, DC, residents the right to vote in presidential elections. He had me work on legal issues concerning home rule for the District of Columbia.

While I worked for the Jones, Day, Reavis and Pogue law firm, I came into contact with several African American lawyers who worked in prestigious white-shoe firms. They started the Lawyers Study Group to counsel minority lawyers who were working in these firms as summer associates. Their mission was to educate us on how to navigate these firms and succeed. Among these lawyers who were very generous with their time were J. Clay Smith at Arent Fox, Vincent Cohen at Hogan and Hartson, Wesley Williams at Covington and Burling, and Fredrick Abramson at Sachs, Greenbaum, and Taylor.

My third year at Harvard Law was my most eventful there. I joined Volunteer Defenders, a law school clinical program in which law students represented indigent criminal defendants charged with misdemeanor offenses in the district courts in Boston, including Dorchester, a largely African American community. One of my memorable clients was a young African American man who was charged with carrying a pistol without a license. I tried the case without a jury before Judge Troy, a judge who had had disciplinary problems and was rumored to be racially biased. I won an acquittal from Judge Troy, presenting the defense that my client had found the gun, and when he was stopped, he was on his way to a police station to turn it in, virtually the only viable defense for a defendant charged with possession of a gun without a license.

My client and his family were overjoyed with his acquittal, and I was praised for my legal talent at a party at his house. This experience was most gratifying and confirmed my thinking regarding the kind of law I wanted to practice, a practice that would take me into court where I could develop and exercise litigation skills. Therefore, I declined the offer that was made to me by Jones Day to join the firm as an associate and accepted the offer to join the US Attorney's Office in the District of Columbia

8 CHAPTER
UNITED STATES ATTORNEYS OFFICE

I did not return for my law school graduation exercises. Instead, I immediately started studying for the bar exam, something I had planned on doing immediately after graduation. I started even earlier and with extra vigor when I was told by Herbert Dixon and Francis "Frenchie" Smith, two recent black graduates of the Georgetown Law Center who had secured jobs with the company that offered the bar review course, that there had been a recent spate of Harvard Law graduates who had flunked the DC Bar. Since I would not be able to start as an assistant United States attorney, a position I secured during my third year in law school, until I was a member of the bar, I was particularly anxious to do all that I could to pass. Toward that end, I reverted to my Princeton study habits, doing little else from May 1973 until July 1973 than study. I was not surprised that I passed as my strategy of memorizing the three-volume bar review course books proved to be a sure way to success.

During the summer of 1973, I—along with the rest of the country—was riveted by the televised proceedings of the Watergate hearings. I witnessed how our democracy deals with abuse of power by a president. I also witnessed how politicians became statesmen as did Howard Baker and Sam Erwin and others who put country before self-interest and party. I followed closely the courageous decisions made by Elliott Richardson and William Ruckelshaus to refuse to fire Archibald Cox as Nixon had ordered and the honesty of Alexander Butterfield in disclosing that the conversations of President Nixon in the Oval Office revealing that the president was part of a criminal conspiracy had been recorded and the tapes had been preserved. I was transfixed by news reports of what had been discovered by Carl Bernstein and Bob Woodward from Deep Throat about the nefarious activity of the Watergate burglars on behalf of CREEP, the Committee to Re-Elect the President, led by G. Gordon Liddy. Of particular interest to me was the steadfastness of Judge John Sirica in making rulings that established that the president of the United States is not above the law.

I can only hope that there will be current-day politicians who will stand up and become statesmen when dealing with the revelations that are sure to come regarding Donald Trump's relationship with America's enemies, including Russia. Does anyone really believe that he and his campaign for the presidency does not have financial entanglements with Russia and other lugubrious relationships that are entirely unseemly and inappropriate for the president of the United States.

I was sworn into the bar and took the oath of office as an Assistant United States attorney in December 1973. I was presented with a commission signed by Elliot Richardson, but ironically, it had to be replaced with one that had been signed by Robert Bork in December 1973 after Richardson resigned rather than carrying out Richard Nixon's order to fire Archibald Cox.

The oath of office as an Assistant US Attorney was administered to me by Judge William C. Pryor, a judge on the Superior Court of the District of Columbia. On the same day, three other recent law school graduates who would become personal friends were also sworn in as an Assistant United States Attorneys: Mark Tuohey, with whom I would share an office in the misdemeanor trial section and would become president of the DC Bar, Bernard Paneta who became a well-regarded and successful lawyer in private practice in El Paso, Texas, and David Addis, who became a flamboyant and successful businessman with a flourishing business in Brazil. Regrettably David chose to end our friendship due to his objecting to my filing suit seeking to have Donald Trump's liquor license in the District of Columbia revoked on the grounds that Trump cannot meet the law's requirement that a person who seeks to have such a license must of good character. I was surprised to learn of David's objection since if there is anything that is crystal clear it is that Donald Trump, by any measure, does not have good character.

My first assignment in the US Attorneys Office was in the misdemeanor trial section. While there, I prosecuted criminal offenses the punishment for which the maximum sentence was no more than one year in jail and or a fine of $1,000. I prosecuted assault, drug possession, petit larceny, and prostitution cases, several involving Antoinette "Six-Pack," a pretty young woman who— despite being sternly lectured by several judges about her conduct and placed on probation several times—always returned to ply her trade on the corner of Fourteenth and L Street, NW, always between the hours of 9:00 p.m. and 2:00 a.m., just outside the entrance to the People's drugstore.

The almost three years I spent in the US Attorneys Office were among the most gratifying of my legal career. I represented a client, the United States, that was duty bound to seek justice—not just win—and to do so in a fair manner. Thus, I always felt energized and even righteous when I would stand before a jury, which I did often, and say, "Ladies and gentlemen of the jury, my name is Henry H. Kennedy Jr., and I represent the people of the United States and the District of Columbia." Also, I was not required to fill out time records in which I would record what I did in ten-minute increments (now such records are kept in in increments of six minutes) as I would be required to do at Jones Day or any other law firm.

My most momentous cases while in the misdemeanor trial section were assigned to me directly by the US Attorney, Earl Silbert, a tremendous lawyer. One was a solicitation case brought against a partner at the prestigious law firm of Covington and Burling. The young partner claimed that he was just exchanging pleasantries with the scantily clad undercover policewoman walking the streets near the corridor where it was widely known that prostitutes conducted their business. This street was nowhere near streets leading to and from Covington. I interviewed both the lawyer and the undercover officer regarding what happened. Though I was opposed to criminalizing efforts to procure sex for money, the "oldest profession," I determined that the partner had broken the law prohibiting such conduct and signed off on his prosecution.

Another sensitive prosecution was of two white Metropolitan Police Officers who initially had managed to evade prosecution on allegations that they had assaulted a black man detained at the DC Jail without cause. The young African American charged with a drug offense alleged that two white Metropolitan Police Officers maced him while he was in a police cell for no reason other than that they thought he was being disrespectful to them. He reported the attack to employees at the DC Jail where he was being held who reported the incident to other MPD officers. These officers wrote up a report and brought the allegations to the US Attorney's office. The case was "no papered," the term used in the US Attorney's Office to indicate that a prosecutor was exercising his prosecutorial discretion to not bring a case.

Richard "Dickie" Tynes, an African American prosecutor in the grand jury section of the office where the decision to no paper had been made, was of the view that this exercise of prosecutorial discretion was unwarranted. Further, he doubted that other assistants would take on the Metropolitan Police Department in favor of a young African American male charged with a drug offense. It should be appreciated that prosecutors have a bond with, and appreciation for, police officers, normally their key witnesses in most prosecutions, more than most people. He therefore recommended that the case be assigned to me after he took the case to a Grand Jury that authorized a prosecution.

I prosecuted the two officers before a jury in a trial presided over by Judge David Norman. A remarkable man blinded when he was a boy, Norman was chief of the US Department of Justice's civil rights division in the Nixon administration before his appointment to the superior court. The two police officers were represented by an experienced defense attorney, Charles Schultz. Following a hard-fought trial, a jury convicted the officers of assault, a just result based on the assault victim's testimony, which was corroborated by evidence that the mace containers carried by the officers had been discharged and weighed considerably less than they weighed before their discharge on the day of the assault. I was so pleased that my father was present for the trial and return of the jury's verdict. Dad had often experienced disrespectful and inappropriate conduct at the hands of police officers without their being reprimanded or otherwise called to account. I know he was pleased to see these police officers brought to justice.

Most of my time in the US Attorneys Office was spent in the appellate section, where I briefed and argued cases, most of them criminal, before the United States court of appeals for the DC Circuit and the District of Columbia court of appeals. The head of the appellate section was John A. Terry, an extraordinary man who, following his time in the US Attorneys Office, served on the District of Columbia court of appeals. A very demanding supervisor, Terry rigorously reviewed the first drafts of the briefs of assistants and provided detailed instructions for modifications generously scrawled in red ink markings referred to by his underlings as "Jatters."

My most interesting appellate case involved the conviction of a young man of first-degree murder of his mother by brutally stabbing her without any known motive. The defendant had been suffering from mental illness for years and was living with his mother who had been taking care of him. In a no-jury trial, Judge Charles Richey rejected the defendant's insanity defense in the face of substantial expert testimony supporting the defense and a factual scenario which spoke for itself in favor of that defense. Composing a lengthy memorandum pointing out how the trial judge had not articulated a basis for rejecting the insanity defense, I unsuccessfully attempted to persuade John Terry and Earl Silbert to confess error on appeal. They explained that it would not do for the government to have argued one way before Judge Richey and then to reverse course on appeal and say that he erred when he accepted that argument. Specifically, the government would not say that it had wrongly brought a prosecution and then erroneously argued before Judge Richey that the defendant had not carried his burden of proving that his conduct was the product of a mental disease or mental defect.

The defendant was represented on appeal by two lawyers. Nathan Lewin was a well-known and highly respected member of the bar, and Jamie Gorelick who was quickly making a name for herself as a litigator. Jamie was to become deputy attorney general of the United States under Janet Reno and in private practice, for a short period of time, represented President Trump's son-in-law Jared Kushner. An assistant to the solicitor general in the Department of Justice under Solicitors General Archibald Cox and Thurgood Marshall, Lewin had argued twelve cases before the Supreme Court of the United States. Jamie Gorelick graduated from Harvard, where she was a roommate of singer Bonnie Raitt, and the Harvard Law School.

The appeal and oral argument before the United States court of appeals for the DC Circuit were before Judges Warren Burger, David Bazelon, and Edward Tamm. Judge Burger and Judge Bazelon served on the United States court of appeals for the DC Circuit for more than a decade together. It was widely known, at least around the courthouse, that the two were not just professional rivals, but personal antagonists as well. Burger was known for his jurisprudence, which often favored law enforcement. Bazelon, on the other hand, was a nationally recognized advocate for the rights of the mentally ill. His opinion in *Durham v. United States*, 214 F.2d 862 (DC Cir. 1954), which adopted a new criminal insanity test, set off a long clash between the two judges. Under Bazelon's Durham rule, a defendant was excused from criminal responsibility if a jury found that the unlawful act was "the product of mental disease or mental defect" rather than the product of an "irresistible impulse" (which was the old test). Burger found the Durham rule deeply objectionable, and this was one of the serious disagreements the two would have over the course of their careers.

Thus, at oral argument, I stood before a panel of the US court of appeals consisting of two judicial heavyweights, representing the United States and arguing a position that I personally did not think was correct against bright and experienced lawyers who were advocating a position with which I agreed. I said about two sentences during oral argument before Bazelon and Burger began to wage verbal war against each other using me to articulate the points they wished to establish. When oral argument was completed, I was as emotionally spent as any time in my life up to that point.

The DC Circuit affirmed the conviction, Burger and Tamm in the majority and Bazelon in dissent. I wholeheartedly agreed with the dissent.

9 CHAPTER
UNITED STATES
MAGISTRATE

I first met Fredrick Abramson in the summer between my second and third year in law school. Fred was a remarkable man and was a founder of the Lawyers Study Group. I had been in the United States Attorneys Office for two years when Fred approached me and inquired whether I might be interested in filling a vacancy that had just been created when Arthur Burnett stepped down as United States Magistrate. I demurred initially as I was altogether satisfied with how my career was progressing in the United States Attorneys Office. I ended up applying for the United States Magistrate position, however, and was completely surprised when the United States district judges appointed me. I was twenty-eight years old.

Because I was not very experienced, I devoted an unusual amount of time to learning my job. That learning began the day after my wedding to my first wife. We went to New York City for our honeymoon, and I shadowed an experienced and well-regarded United States Magistrate for two days.

I served as United States Magistrate from 1976 until 1979. During that time, I presided over numerous extraordinarily interesting proceedings, including the criminal pretrial proceedings for Linwood Gray, a young African American charged with directing the largest cocaine operation ever prosecuted in the District of Columbia and one of the largest in the country. Gray's organization was charged with moving thousands of pounds of cocaine from the Middle East to cities in the eastern United States.

Linwood Gray and his wife were brought before me after their arrest by the FBI to determine the amount of the bond—if any—they would be required to post pending their trial. Their capture followed an investigation that had lasted several years. I imposed a multimillion-dollar bond on each of them and seized the funds in their several bank accounts, thereby ensuring that they would be detained before their trial. Gray was represented by Kenneth Michael Robinson, a flamboyant lawyer with a thick southern accent.

After I imposed bond on his clients, Robinson filed a motion to reduce the bonds, and at a hearing on the motion, vigorously argued that it should be granted. At the hearing, Robinson was as flamboyant as ever, arguing that the government's claims that Gray was a heroin kingpin who enforced his rule over the alleged drug ring by violence were based on "unsubstantiated, uncharged, and unproven allegations."

When Gray heard me deny the motion for a reduction of his bond, Gray blurted out, "Your name is Kennedy. You look like Martin Luther King, but you are just a rebel. You are a George Wallace." After the hearing, a division of the United States Marshal Service, which specializes in detecting threats to the judiciary, listened to a tape of the proceedings and explained that each of the persons Gray had mentioned had been shot.

The fear that Gray had intended to issue a death threat was confirmed shortly afterward when Barry Leibowitz, the assistant United States attorney assigned to handle the pretrial proceedings in Gray's case, and had argued against reducing his bond, was shot and wounded in the parking lot just outside the US Courthouse while standing near my car. No one was ever arrested and charged with the shooting, but it was widely accepted that Gray was behind it. Gray's threat prompted the Marshal Service to provide me bodyguards for several weeks following Gray's proceedings before me.

A few years after Gray's conviction, he attempted to kill his lawyer. At some point during the proceedings leading up to his trial, Gray transferred the house in which he lived with his wife and child to Kenneth Robinson for payment of his legal fees. After Gray's conviction for tax evasion, Robinson went about the business of evicting Gray's wife from the house in order to liquidate it. Through intermediaries, Gray warned Robinson not to evict his wife, and when Robinson persisted in doing so, he attempted to have him killed. While Robinson was severely wounded, he survived the shooting.

Gray's threat was not the last time my life would be threatened by a criminal defendant. When I was on the D.C. Superior Court, I tried a man charged with attempted murder. I sentenced him to a lengthy prison term, which he tried to have reduced many times. Each time, I denied his sentence reduction motion. The last denial incited him, and he wrote me a letter telling me that when he got out of prison he was going to "step to me," an obvious threat. I notified the US Marshal service and the FBI, who began an investigation by first interviewing him at the Lorton Reformatory.

FBI agents reported to me that the prisoner who had threatened me had himself been threatened by several of his fellow prisoners who liked me because while I had incarcerated them, they thought my sentence had been fair and that I respectfully had explained why I imposed the sentences that I did. According to the agents, this was a first.

Another extraordinary proceeding in which I was involved while a United States magistrate stemmed from signing a warrant that authorized the FBI to search the offices of the Church of Scientology. The church was long suspected of engaging in unlawful conduct in furtherance of the church's alleged efforts to undermine public confidence in government and public officials. On July 3, 1977, close to midnight, lawyers from the Department of Justice arrived at my apartment and along with FBI agents waited outside of my apartment while I reviewed the one-hundred-page affidavit that was submitted to support the government's request for a warrant. The assistant US attorney who accompanied the FBI agents explained that the warrant was being sought in conjunction with the seeking of a warrant to search Scientology offices in Europe by Interpol, and that Interpol and US authorities intended to execute the warrants on both continents at the same time. I signed the warrant, which became the subject of a motion to suppress the evidence that was seized pursuant to it. The church claimed that pages of the warrant that had been returned after the search and seizure of items at the church's offices were not the same pages that had been submitted along with the affidavit supporting the search warrant for my review and that the pages that I reviewed, unlike the ones allegedly replacing them, did not adequately limit the scope of the search that the warrant permitted.

At a hearing on the motion to suppress the evidence, I testified regarding what was presented to me for my review. I explained that my practice was to initial each page of the affidavit presented to support the warrant but not the warrant itself. Judge Bryant, a judge respected and admired above all others, curtly said, "That was not good enough." That comment, coming from Judge Bryant hurt, even though I knew he was wrong.

Judge Bryant granted the motion to suppress, which ruling on appeal was unanimously reversed. I felt no vindication by the appellate court's ruling, however, as it was not in my eyes a substitute for the approval of a judge I greatly admired.

10 CHAPTER
ALTOMEASE

I met Altomease again shortly after I was appointed United States Magistrate. I had met her years earlier when she was introduced to me by her then-husband, Francis "Frenchie" Smith. Frenchie and Al met when she was a freshmen at Goucher College in Towson Maryland and he was a sophomore at Johns Hopkins in Baltimore. They married soon after she graduated from Goucher and he was a second-year law student at the Georgetown Law Center.

When he introduced me to Al, Frenchie was working at the DC Public Defender Service and I was an Assistant United States attorney. Frenchie and I were very active in the Young Lawyers Section of the DC Bar and we each wanted to distinguish ourselves among the predominantly white group. Therefore, when we attended YLS meetings, we each strove mightily to show that we were the smartest person in the room. This invariably caused both of us to find something more to say following the other's comment—no matter how fulsome the comment or suggestion on any topic.

One of the efforts of the Young Lawyer Section was to support legislation that would permit DC citizens to register to vote at the same time they registered their automobiles, known at the time as a "motor voter law." When this law was passed by the city council, the Young Lawyer Section had a party in a town house in southwest Washington to celebrate. It was at this party that Frenchie introduced me to Al. I greeted her and attempted to exchange pleasantries, but she would have none of it. She responded with one-word utterances, and her body language communicated that she would just as soon be relieved of having to respond at all to my attempts to be cordial. I was truly taken aback and said to myself, "Those two deserve each other."

Five years later, when I was separated from my first wife, I ran into

Charles Wagner who had worked with me in the United States Attorneys Office. He was walking along Pennsylvania Avenue, and we stopped to catch up a bit. He learned I was separated and suggested that I join him and his wife Annice, the then Chief Judge of the DC Court of Appeals, for sailing on their boat, the *Succubus,* so named for a Lilin demon in female form, or supernatural entity in folklore (traced back to medieval legend) that appears in dreams and takes the form of a woman in order to seduce men, usually through sexual activity.

When we parted that day, I did not expect to hear from Charles again regarding the idea of my joining him and Annice for sailing, but sure enough, he called three days later and asked whether I was available for sailing the following weekend when it was expected to be unseasonably warm for November. He said that I could bring a date—or Annice could arrange for a blind date. He told me that Annice had several women friends who were pleasing to look at and had good heads on their shoulders. Although I was dating a very attractive young woman at the time, I told Charles I would welcome meeting one of Annice's friends.

Two days later, Charles called to tell me the details for the sailing trip, which would be off the coast of Solomons Island on the eastern shore of Maryland. He informed me that my date would be Altomease Smith and that Betty and Harold Cushenberry would be joining us. The Cushenberrys were law school classmates of Al's, and Betty had worked for Annice when Annice was DC's People's Counsel. I did not recognize Al's name initially and thought, *That's a strange name.*

A few days later, I was crossing Seventh Street in front of Hecht's Department store when it dawned on me that the woman who was to be my date on the sailing outing was the woman who had been so ungracious and unfriendly years earlier. *That bitch!* I was stuck. I had already committed to going on the trip and had asked Annice to get me the date.

When I arrived at Charles and Annice's house and had my first contact with Al in five years, my worst fear was confirmed. As I approached Al, Charles said, "I am sure you know each other."

It was clear that Al was not going to respond, so after an awkward period of silence, I said, "Yes, I know Altomease."

With this, Al cheerily piped up, "Yes, I know Henry." Much later, Al confessed that she was wary that I may not have remembered her and waited until I acknowledged her before she would acknowledge me. She admitted that she would have said that she did not know me if I had said that I didn't know her.

Surprisingly, after our awkward introduction, our time together on the *Succubus* was quite enjoyable. The three couples, all being lawyers, talked about legal and social policy issues over good food and drink. When it was my turn to take the tiller of the *Succubus*, Al fed me bite-sized pieces of food by inserting the morsels into my mouth. It seemed to me that she was doing so quite happily and pushed the morsels deeper into my mouth and for much longer than necessary. I sensuously licked her fingers each time.

After a lovely afternoon sailing, we returned to DC. Al and I rode in the back of the Cushenberrys' car. Immediately after we arrived at the Wagners' home at about six thirty, in the presence of Harold and Betty and Charles and Annice, I told Altomease that I had had a very good time and asked her to have dinner with me.

Al demurred, stating that she already had other plans for the evening.

I kicked myself for so plainly showing my attraction and felt embarrassed for having made my feelings known in the presence of others and having my invitation so unceremoniously turned down. Though I had found her attractive, witty, and smart, I regretted that my embarrassment would result in my never seeing her again as I would never ask her out again.

Luckily, Annice and Betty sensed my negative reaction to Al's turning down my invitation and the next day counseled her to call me. Against her natural inclination not to call any man for social reasons, she followed the advice of Betty and Annice and called. Known in Kennedy family lore as "the great beg back," Al earnestly told me how much she enjoyed our time together sailing, regretted that she was unable to accept my invitation, and fervently hoped that we would see each other again soon.

Al's phone call soothed my pique somewhat, but I waited two weeks before calling her. I invited her to dinner on a Sunday evening, clearly messaging that I had other plans for Friday and Saturday evening, the prime date nights.

Al told me that she had to go to Philadelphia on Sunday evening in order to attend a business meeting the following Monday. Sensing, correctly, that I would not take kindly to her again declining my dinner invitation she blurted out, "what about breakfast, lunch, brunch? That's it-brunch!" That's it—brunch!" I was thoroughly amused by her pressured speech indicating her awareness of what was at stake. We agreed on brunch.

We began to date, and the rest is history—a very gratifying one filled with love and good fortune resulting in the creation of a beautiful family of which we are immensely proud, more so than of any of our separate accomplishments.

Annual family Christmas brunch at the Four Seasons Hotel in Georgetown, Washington, DC.

11 CHAPTER
SUPERIOR COURT

Judges of the DC Superior Court are the only judges of a court of general jurisdiction in this country who are appointed by the president of the United States and confirmed by the United States Senate. This is because the District Columbia has a peculiar status, a jurisdiction over which the Congress has ultimate authority while a city government exercises "home rule" to a significant extent. I was appointed to the superior court by President Jimmy Carter on December 17, 1979, after having served as a United States magistrate for three years.

My confirmation hearings were held before the Senate's Committee on Government Operations. The committee was chaired by Thomas Eagleton who was very supportive of my appointment even though I was only twenty-nine years old. As he explained at my hearing, he too was very young, thirty-two years old when he was elected attorney general of Missouri and thirty-six when he was elected the state's lieutenant governor.

Eagleton also suffered from depression throughout his life, resulting in several hospitalizations, which were kept secret from the public but proved to be his undoing when during his campaign to become vice president of the United States on the Democratic ticket with Walter Mondale the public became aware that he had received electroconvulsive therapy.

J. Clay Smith, a fellow Asbury Methodist church member and a well-regarded professor of law at the Howard University Law School introduced me to the committee and spoke on my behalf at the hearing. I was unanimously voted out of committee and did not receive any nay votes on the floor of the Senate.

Superior court judges are assigned to the divisions of the court—criminal, civil, family, landlord and tenant—for periods of time that last from six to twelve months. Selected judges, those with experience in probate law, are assigned to the tax and probate division. Because the superior court is a court of general jurisdiction that serves an international city, its judges preside over a wide variety of cases—from murder and rape criminal cases to landlord and tenant cases and disputes over complex commercial transactions.

One of the most challenging assignments for a superior court judge is to be assigned to the family division. In this division, judges handle domestic and neglect and abuse cases. In these cases, the governing standard for a judge regarding the treatment of children is "what is in the best interest of the child." This seemingly straightforward standard in truth is one that is anything but.

A scenario I faced all too often involved a child who I had to remove from his home because of the mother's neglect and sometimes abuse stemming from drug addiction. I earnestly would challenge the mother to address her drug problem so that she would be able to care for her child properly. In the meantime, the child would be placed with a family, some desperately desiring to have a child to parent, that was able to offer the child a safe environment where the child would be able to thrive. Often the members of this family were more educated and well off financially and otherwise than members of the birth family. This family would bond with the child, love it just as if it were the family's biological offspring, and then would seek to adopt the child. The birth mother in the meantime would courageously and successfully address her drug problem. In the end, the question was which family would serve the child's best interest. In making that judgment, should it make a difference that the two families were of different races? What if the family that was not the child's birth family were two gay men? These cases were agonizing, required the wisdom of Solomon, and often turned on the most exacting exercise of fact-finding.

My colleagues on the superior court were hardworking and caring jurists. I remain enormously proud to have served with them. One outstanding and memorable colleague was Luke Moore, one of Dad's good friends with whom he worked at the US Post Office before Luke went to law school. Dad and several other black postal workers would cover for Luke while he studied for the bar. As a judge, it was Moore's seemingly infinite patience with lawyers and witnesses that made him known in the halls of superior court as "forever Moore."

Moore grew up in the segregated South, attended public schools, and entered LeMoyne-Owen College, a historically black college in Memphis, before he was drafted into the US Army. He served in the Ninety-Second Infantry Division in Italy. All the enlisted men in his division were African American. Moore finished college on the GI Bill, graduating with honors in 1949 from Howard University.

While attending Georgetown University Law School, Moore worked nights as a mail distributor with the Railway Mail Service. After many experiences with racism, who could complain if Luke had been left by years of segregation with scars on his personality or baggage of prejudice or a bias in his judgment or heart? But Luke had none of these. By some miracle and strength of character, Luke rose above the natural order of his environment to soar to the height of being a person who truly bore no malice or prejudice or bias toward anyone. Instead, he truly cared for and about the welfare of everyone with whom he came into contact. It is no surprise to anyone who knew Luke that he died of a heart attack on a Thanksgiving Day while raking the leaves in the yard of an elderly neighbor to his second wife.

The most interesting and consequential case I handled as a superior court judge was a criminal case to which I was assigned in 1990, *United States v. Kevin Porter*. Porter was charged with raping the fourteen-year-old sister of his girlfriend. In this case, for the first time in the District of Columbia and one of the first anywhere in the United States, the prosecution sought to admit deoxyribonucleic acid (DNA) evidence, a new type of forensic evidence that had been developed through cutting-edge technology and scientific discovery that was first used by British law enforcement officers in 1988 to identify the perpetrator of two murders in Leicester, England. The investigation and prosecution of these murders were the subject of James Wambaugh's best-selling book *The Blooding*.

DNA evidence is an outgrowth of the pioneering work of American James Watson and Francis Crick of Great Britain. They received the Nobel Prize for discovering the chemical structure of the DNA molecule, the biological unit of life upon which DNA evidence is based. Eleven other criminal cases pending in the court in which the government similarly sought to admit this evidence were assigned to me to decide its admissibility.

The government sought to admit expert testimony developed by the FBI that the DNA extracted from semen specimens taken from the sheet on the bed where the rape had allegedly taken place matched the DNA taken from Porter's blood and that the probability of a coincidental match between two unrelated black males with this DNA profile was no lower than one in thirty million. The DNA evidence was thus intended to corroborate the complainant's expected identification of Porter as her assailant and to demonstrate that it was extremely unlikely that someone other than Porter had committed the crime. Porter asked the court to exclude the proffered evidence.

The science underling DNA evidence is mind-bogglingly complicated.

Embedded within the nucleus of virtually every cell of each human being's body are forty-six rod-shaped chromosomes. Half of these chromosomes are inherited from one's mother and half are inherited from one's father. Each chromosome has the shape of a twisted ladder or spiral staircase. The bannisters of this staircase are made of phosphates and sugars, while the steps, or rungs, consist of base pairs, or pairs of amino acids bound together in consistent unalterable fashion. A single DNA molecule—itself not a very large entity—contains about three billion base pairs. Each person's DNA is unique.

The first step in the process used to make a DNA comparison is to isolate segments of the DNA molecule by a molecular biological process called *electrophoresis*. The resulting segments are compared to determine if they match, that is whether they are within a predetermined range that could signify that they indeed are the same and come from the same person. Finally, a mathematical formula is employed, the product rule, to determine the possibility that what seem to be a match and comes from the same person is merely coincidental.

When I was assigned the Porter case, I immediately thought back to the difficulty I had understanding the science of DNA while taking biology at Princeton, the class that dissuaded me from pursuing my aspiration to become a physician. In that class, I sat in a chair that bore a small brass tag indicating that it once had been occupied by Albert Einstein. How ironic that I would be making a decision that would require a comprehensive understanding of the science of DNA and would doubtless influence the decisions of judges around the country regarding the admissibility of this new evidence, including Judge Lance Ito, who presided over "the trial of the century" and perhaps the most publicized trial in history, which was underway in California, *California v. Orenthal J. Simpson.*

Porter was represented by dedicated, energetic, and smart lawyers, Ronald Goodbread and Francis D'Antuono. James Klein, a superb lawyer with the DC Public Defender Service, was allowed to intervene to oppose this evidence as amicus curiae. These lawyers were neither overwhelmed nor intimidated by the government's resources and were committed to doing whatever was necessary to exclude have this new forensic evidence, which cost several millions of dollars to develop, excluded. In other jurisdictions, when defense counsel were confronted with the prosecution motions to admit DNA evidence they were steamrolled by the government's superior resources and the evidence was admitted without being truly contested. I was extremely proud of the work done by these lawyers who were working, with little compensation, to ensure that this new powerful evidence was thoroughly vetted.

Some of defense counsel's arguments against the admissibility of the proffered DNA evidence resonated with me from the very outset. For example, I was immediately suspicious of a premise underlying the government's arguments regarding how to calculate coincidental match probabilities.

The government posited that it made a difference in calculating this part of its evidence that the databases it used to make DNA comparisons were properly and necessarily divided on the basis of "race" and that it was scientifically acceptable in creating the racial databases to accept a person's self-identification as to his or her race.

Even without considering the views of eminent population and human geneticist, as I eventually did, I knew these assumptions were anything but scientific. First, there are no specific racial genes, that is, there is no sequence of genes that is unique to blacks, whites, Asians, or any other racial grouping. To the contrary "race" is entirely a social and cultural construct, not a scientifically grounded fact. In the United States, for example, a person is identified as being of the Negro, black, or African American "race," even if his ancestry is overwhelmingly "white," if he has just "one drop" of "black blood." Ironically, this construct virtually ensures the extinction of the white "race." There are more genetic differences intra-racially than interracially.

Further, one's self-identification of his race is fraught with problems. The reality is that one may not know his or her race. Undoubtedly, there are thousands of people, perhaps more, who believe they are white because of their appearance but may not know that their great-grandfather who had the external appearance of being white was in fact black, making them, as defined by American convention, black as well. Moreover, even if a person did know that he was black, he might, as many African Americans have done, pass for white. The opposite is also true, though nowhere near as frequent. I personally know of a white family who passed for black, as well as a fellow white student at Princeton who transformed himself into being black and today would so identify himself.

I conducted a twenty-day hearing during which I heard from eight expert witnesses who testified regarding the several disciplines that contribute to an understanding of DNA evidence: human and population genetics, organic chemistry, biology, mathematics, and forensic science. There were 110 exhibits introduced during the hearing, and I received more than 1,300 pages of briefs.

Following the hearing, I issued an order accompanied by a ninety-three-page opinion in which I held that the government's methodology for determining that a DNA sample taken from the crime scene matched the DNA of Porter was widely accepted within the scientific community. I determined as well, however, that the statistical methodology employed by the government to arrive at the possibility of a random or coincidental match was the subject of fundamental disagreement among geneticists. For this reason, applying the governing standard set forth in the venerable *United States v. Frye* decision—which requires that before new scientific evidence is admitted at a criminal trial, it must find general acceptance in the scientific community—I denied the government's motion to admit its DNA evidence.

My opinion described the substantial controversy among distinguished scientists as to the soundness of certain assumptions on which the coincidental match probabilities calculation were based. Foremost among the scientists who questioned the validity of the method used to determine coincidental match probabilities was Richard C. Lewontin, a leader in developing the mathematical basis of population genetics and evolutionary theory. Lewontin pioneered the application of techniques from molecular biology, such as gel electrophoresis, to questions of genetic variation and evolution. Lewontin's views were corroborated by a study conducted by the National Research Council while Porter's case was pending.

On appeal, the District of Columbia court of appeals, Frank Schwelb, a fine jurist with whom I had served on superior court, writing for the majority, affirmed each of my factual and legal rulings, but he remanded the case in view of the National Research Council Report that had been completed during the pendency of the appeal so I could determine whether the DNA evidence "should be admitted on the basis of a probability calculation for which the requisite consensus may now exist." Judge Julia Mack wrote a dissenting opinion.

Bound to follow the instruction of the court of appeals, I scheduled another hearing to determine whether there then existed the relevant scientific consensus as defined in the court of appeals' opinion.

The dissent of Judge Julia Cooper Mack displayed a clearer understanding of the problems presented by DNA evidence than the majority and a wise perspective regarding its admissibility as evidence in criminal cases and its significance for the entirety of the criminal justice system. Judge Mack perceptively observed,

[A]part from the considerations of Frye, from an administrative viewpoint, our criminal justice system cannot ignore the cost of widespread use of DNA typing (expected to run into the tens of millions of dollars, a year). The fact that DNA evidence might obviate trials in some cases may be cause for assurance or fear, depending upon one's point of view.

Man's "search for truth" is a never-ending odyssey. The ultimate issue here, however, is not whether the search for truth should be employed to determine whether Mr. Porter is guilty or innocent of a sexual assault on a complaining witness, but rather whether a hastily developed two-part methodology which reeks of scientific controversy in critical respect, can be employed summarily to undermine a system of individual justice, carefully and painfully crafted over the centuries.

Having heard from the scientists called as expert witnesses during the twenty-day hearing I had held two years earlier, I knew that at any future hearing where only experts would be called (and paid for) by the prosecution and the defense I would hear testimony with a spin that favored the party that called them. I therefore decided to take the unusual step of calling my own expert witness, one who would not tailor his testimony to favor any particular outcome other than one grounded in science. Having read about the high regard in which Dr. Eric Lander was held by human population geneticists of all stripes, including James Watson and my brother who had been selected the year after Lander as a Rhodes scholar, I decided to attempt to engage him as the court's expert.

Lander attended Princeton University, and he graduated in 1978 as valedictorian. He then attended the University of Oxford as a Rhodes scholar and wrote his doctoral thesis on algebraic coding theory and symmetric block design.

I reached Dr. Lander by telephone and told him what I was attempting to do and the importance of the issue I faced. He demurred, indicating that his work as head of MIT's Whitehead Institute and scheduled appearances at several conferences, some out of them country, would prevent his giving testimony at a hearing in the District of Columbia. I would not relent and pulled out all of the stops.

Referring to him as a fellow Princetonian, speaking of my brother's high regard of him, and reminding him of our University's informal motto "Princeton in the nation's service and in the service of all nations," I told him that in view of his time constraints, I would hold the hearing in Boston—where he worked and lived—and would limit the time he would be called upon to testify to no more than one hour. With this assurance, Dr. Lander agreed to be the court's expert witness at a hearing that would be conducted in the historic Suffolk County Courthouse in Boston.

At the hearing, I questioned Dr. Lander first and limited the lawyers' questioning of him to twenty minutes apiece. As it turns out, following my questioning, the lawyers had very few questions.

Fortuitously, immediately after the hearing, Lander had lunch with

Dr. Bruce Budowle, who had traveled to Boston from Washington to attend the hearing. Dr. Bruce Budowle had joined the research unit at the FBI Laboratory Division in 1983 to carry out research, development, and validation of methods for forensic biological analysis. At lunch, Dr. Lander and Dr. Budowle discussed the issues that divided geneticists regarding DNA evidence and eventually coauthored an article that appeared in *Nature*, a prominent peer-review journal. This article once and for all put to rest the controversy surrounding the forensic uses of DNA evidence given the immense respect accorded its authors, particularly Dr. Lander, as they endorsed a methodology for determining coincidental match probabilities that scientists could agree on.

Following the hearing, I wrote another opinion finding that a conservative methodology for calculating match probabilities—one determined by the National Research Council—would find general acceptance in the scientific community.

California State Judge Lance Ito who was handling the murder prosecution of O. J. Simpson called my chambers several times in the months before my second hearing to inquire when I would make my decision because his decisions regarding the admissibility of DNA evidence in the Simpson case would be strongly influenced by my anticipated ruling as had been my first ruling. Immediately after issuing my opinion, I informed Judge Ito. Because of my opinion and Ito's evident determination to follow it, Simpson's lawyers dropped their attack on the admissibility of DNA evidence. Instead, they focused their challenge to the evidence on how the police had mishandled it at the crime scene and its chain of custody.

Porter was convicted principally on the basis of the DNA introduced against him.

Another criminal case I handled as a Superior Court Judge was notable for its unlikely history. It was a burglary prosecution of a young man charged with burglarizing a home in southeast Washington, the poorest area of the city with a heavily predominant black population. The prosecution's main witness testified that she remembered the day of the burglary because at the time of the defendant's entry to her apartment, she was in her kitchen "warming some chitterlings." During slavery, slave owners commonly fed their slaves as cheaply as possible. At hog-butchering time, the best cuts of meat were kept for the master's household and the remainder, such as the hog's intestines (chitterlings, in the African American community, pronounced "chitlins") were given to the slaves.

The defendant, she testified, then burglarized her home and robbed her and other inhabitants of the apartment. The defendant was found guilty by a jury of each of the charges brought against him.

The first unusual aspect of the case's history was the motion for a new trial that was filed shortly after the jury delivered its guilty verdict. It seems that one of the jurors had squirreled a pint of liquor into the jury deliberation room and proceeded to imbibe it until he was past drunk. Like a character in one of Richard Pryor's stand-up comedy routines, he became belligerent and behaved in such a way as to make rational deliberation extremely difficult. As it turns out, he, like the other eleven jurors, voted to convict but only after offering to kick another juror's ass for speaking to him in a way that he found unacceptable.

I denied the motion for a new trial, which became the basis of the defendant's appeal of his conviction to the District of Columbia Court of Appeals. The appellate court affirmed the conviction, leading to the defendant seeking a writ of certiorari before the United States Supreme Court.

In order to gain a writ of certiorari, four justices must vote to grant it. As it turns out, the defendant's petition was reviewed by my brother—one of Justice Thurgood Marshall's four law clerks, a post he had obtained after clerking for Judge J. Skelly Wright, the liberal lion of the United States Court of Appeals for the DC Circuit. Randy penned a long memorandum to Justice Marshall expressing that because his brother was the trial judge below whose ruling the defendant was seeking to overturn, he should not be recommending whether the writ should issue.

Justice Marshall, in his inimical way, wrote on the memo he returned to Randy: "Randy, I am the judge—not you." The conviction stood.

Another case was that of a young man who was charged with the homicide of an infant. The infant had been left in the care of the young man by his live-in girlfriend who had left their apartment to look for work. After feeding the baby, the child started crying uncontrollably. When the child continued to cry after the young man had done everything he knew how to do to alleviate whatever was causing the infant to cry, he struck the infant with his fist in frustration. When the child lost consciousness, the young man called for emergency help. The baby was taken to the Washington Hospital Center for treatment, but it died shortly after arriving at the hospital.

The young man pled guilty to involuntary manslaughter. The prosecution argued that the man should receive the maximum sentence: five years. The defense argued that he should be given probation pointing out that he had no criminal record, except for a possession of marijuana offense, and urged the court to avoid contributing to two tragedies, the death of the child, for which nothing could be done at that point, and sentencing the defendant to a term of imprisonment that would alter his life for the worse. The defense pointed out that the young man had demonstrated sincere remorse as he had not attempted to flee, had called for help, and indeed had attempted suicide after learning that the child had died.

After agonizing over what a just sentence would be, I sentenced the young man to eighteen months in prison. The sentence was reported in the press and was severely criticized by some for what they considered to be a too lenient sentence. I was roundly denounced in the *National Enquirer*, a supermarket tabloid, as a liberal soft on crime judge. A conservative group, the Washington Legal Foundation, filed a complaint with the District of Columbia Commission on Judicial Disabilities and Tenure, charging that my sentence was outrageously lenient and properly the subject of disciplinary action, including dismissal from the bench. This organization also argued that my association with two organizations, the OARS Foundation, an organization that provided services to ex-convicts so that they might be reintegrated into the community and the Green Door, an organization that provides community-based mental health services to persons suffering with mental illness, was highly inappropriate.

My service on the board of directors of the Green Door was anything but inappropriate. In fact, it was some of the most important community service work I performed while a judge. Brent Henry had served on the board before me and recommended me for the position. At my first meeting of the Green Door board of directors, I met Pamela Harriman. When we were leaving the meeting, I asked if she needed a ride home. She smiled and graciously thanked me for my offer before declining it. About the same time, I noticed a black limousine waiting at the curb manned by a chauffeur who was holding the door for her.

Pamela and I became friends, and I came to understand why powerful men loved her so. She was beyond charming. When talking to her, you had the feeling that you were the most important person in the room and that she never wanted to be distracted from whatever you were saying. She had a way of locking eyes with you so that you never wanted to look away. She was an aerobic listener. When she persisted in calling me Judge after serving together for some time on the Green Door board, I told her that she should call me Henry rather than Judge Kennedy. She sweetly demurred, saying that she loved to use the title when it was associated with someone she liked and respected as much as me.

The Washington Legal Foundation's complaint was dismissed by the Commission on Disability and Tenure as being without merit.

12 CHAPTER
UNITED STATES DISTRICT COURT

When United States District Judge Joyce Hens Green stepped down from the United States District Court for the District of Columbia, I decided to try to secure an appointment to her vacant seat, just as I had done when she left the DC Superior Court. There had been vacancies on the District Court before Green's that I had been encouraged to vie for, but I did not for two reasons. First, when a vacancy occurred about the same time as the expected birth of our second child, a time when both Al and I were immersed in our work and working very long hours, we decided to hire a nanny. Margaret Dean, a citizen of India, was not legally in the United States after overstaying her visa. When Margaret answered our advertisement at the World Bank and came to our house for an interview, it was love at first sight between our older daughter, Morgan, and her. Morgan immediately and without hesitation curled herself up in Margaret's lap, and anyone could see that Margaret had an instant affection for Morgan as well. This connection convinced us that we should hire Margaret even though we knew that anyone who hired an illegal alien would have difficulty gaining Senate confirmation given the "nanny-gate" controversies that had happened months earlier and had doomed President Clinton's nominations of Zoe Baird and Kimba Wood to be Attorney General of the United States.

The second reason I did not seek an appointment was that when vacancies occurred, I was in the throes of a depressive episode and seeking treatment. Thus, I did not have the time or energy to attend to the myriad things one must do to secure a presidential appointment and confirmation while doing my work on the Superior Court.

To become a federal judge is largely serendipitous. There is no road map to the federal bench. Indeed, securing an appointment is like having lightning strike followed by a confirmation process that resembles the process used to make sausage. While the end product may be good, the process used to make it is anything but pretty.

In the District of Columbia, ever since President Carter started the practice, when the president is a Democrat, the District's nonvoting delegate to Congress, Eleanor Holmes Norton, a Democrat, is accorded senatorial courtesy. That is the name for the practice of the president empowering the senior senator from a state, if from the same party of the president, to select persons for appointment to vacancies on the lower federal courts in the senator's state. Delegate Norton established a commission that recommended persons to her whom she then would recommend to the president.

The commission was chaired by Pauline Schneider, a most impressive lawyer, and was comprised of highly regarded lawyers and civic leaders. Following my answering the commission's written questions and appearing before it to do so in person, I, along with two others, received the commission's recommendation.

I was then interviewed by Delegate Norton. When I arrived at her office for my interview, I was met by her chief of staff, Donna Brazile, the extremely personable Democratic Party political operative with whom I easily struck up a conversation. We talked enthusiastically about New Orleans, where she and my father grew up, which is one of my favorite places in the world. We talked about the sights and sounds of the French Quarter, the garden district, jazz, food, and the best places to eat.

Following my interview with Delegate Norton, I returned to my chambers at superior court and soon thereafter received a call from Brazile. She was very kind and said that she thoroughly enjoyed our conversation and hoped that Delegate Norton would recommend me for appointment.

The process that followed was arduous. I completed long questionnaires required by the White House in which I was required to lay bare anything and everything in my background, starting with when I was a child, that might be pertinent to my suitability to hold a lifetime federal judicial post. For example, I was required to reveal the specifics of my medical and financial history and reveal my present and past affiliations with all organizations. This included identifying any organization to which I had ever belonged the membership of which was limited on the basis of race or sex. I was then evaluated by an ABA committee tasked with assessing my qualifications and was determined to be well qualified, the highest ranking that is given a candidate for a federal judicial post. I jumped these hurdles easily, but I was faced with one—thanks to my good friend and superior court colleague Harriet Taylor—that seemed insurmountable.

Harriet and I became good friends very soon after my appointment to the Superior Court. My chambers were next to hers. It was Harriett who, knowing my love of tennis, suggested the vanity plate for my new red Mustang convertible: "4 Hand." Harriett was a wonderful person, extremely bright, and, more than any jurist with whom I have ever been associated, was committed to doing the right thing for the right reason. Harriett was a champion of the poor and powerless and made several rulings that helped ease conditions for the District of Columbia's poor and homeless. She mandated thorough changes for the city government's provision of services for Washington's homeless population which earned her the moniker "the homeless judge."

About the same time as I was negotiating the various steps leading to my hoped for confirmation, Harriett was trying a divorce case involving Sharon Probst, the chief of staff for Orrin Hatch, the senior Republican senator from Utah, who was chairman of the Senate Judiciary Committee. The primary issue in the trial was which parent, Probst or her husband, both lawyers, would be awarded custody of their child. Senator Hatch appeared at the trial and testified on behalf of Probst. Harriett found that while both parents "clearly love their child very much," the father was doing the better job of balancing career and family obligations. Her ruling, which was upheld on appeal, also provided for the payment of child support by Probst to her former husband.

Senator Hatch was furious, an indignation that was heightened by the efforts he had made on Probst's behalf by testifying before Harriett and throwing his considerable weight behind his chief of staff. The Senate Judiciary Committee controls whether a president's appointee to a federal judgeship will be considered by the full Senate, and its chair controls the committee's agenda. Hatch indicated that he would not permit a hearing to be held on my nomination or that of my Superior Court colleague Judge Collen Kollar-Kotelly, who also had been nominated for a seat on the District Court, until Harriet's ruling against Probst was undone.

Fortunately for me, one of my good friends, Paul Friedman—a US District judge with whom I had served in the US Attorneys Office—offered to ask one of his good friends who was a very good friend of Orrin Hatch to intercede on my behalf. David Barrett did so by writing a heartfelt letter of recommendation of me to Hatch.

Unbeknownst to me, others were working behind the scenes on my behalf as well. Republicans were very antagonistic of any nomination by President Clinton who was embroiled in the Monica Lewinsky scandal.

Donna Brazile contacted Armstrong Williams, a Republican friend of hers and a very influential Republican political operative, and highly recommended me. Williams was formerly vice president for a governmental and international affairs public relations firm, B&C Associates, and was good friends of Justice Clarence Thomas whom I knew through Lillian McEwen, a good friend whose daughter, Michelle, is my goddaughter. Williams called Thomas, who vouched for me, and his endorsement was conveyed to the Republican Party.

Efforts also were made on my behalf by my first cousins who live in South Carolina and were anxious to support my nomination. Knowing that Senator Strom Thurmond, South Carolina's long-serving senator was well known for being very attentive to his constituents' concerns, my cousins in a well-crafted letter asked him to support my nomination. One South Carolina cousin, James Price, had been recognized as a standout educator having been awarded a national award recognizing his excellent performance as an elementary school principal. Another, Thaddeus Bell, had been recognized in the field of medicine, and yet another, Gary Bell, was a longtime and accomplished accountant and employee of the state of South Carolina. Shortly after the letter was sent, I received a call from Thurmond's office informing me that Thurmond would support me and would welcome an invitation for him to introduce me to the judiciary committee.

Thurmond had a complicated relationship with blacks. In 1948, the year of my birth, when he ran for the presidency, Thurmond had said "all the laws of Washington and all the bayonets of the army cannot force the Negro into our homes, into our schools, our churches, and our places of recreation and amusement." He fathered a black child in the 1930s. In opposition to the Civil Rights Act of 1957, he conducted the longest filibuster ever by a lone senator, at twenty-four hours and eighteen minutes in length, nonstop. In the 1960s, he opposed the civil rights legislation of 1964 and 1965 to end segregation and enforce the constitutional rights of African American citizens, including the right to vote.

I met Thurmond in person for the first time just before my confirmation hearing. In an ornate room next to the large room in the Senate where the confirmation hearings were to take place, he said, "Judge Kennedy, you have established a good name and reputation. Never do anything to taint them." Thurmond, a former chair of judiciary committee, and Delegate Norton introduced me to the judiciary committee, with Thurmond giving unusually warm and complimentary remarks.

Among the senators at the hearing were Orrin Hatch, Jeff Sessions from Alabama, and John Ashcroft from Missouri. They asked questions regarding some of the hot-button issues of the day for which I had prepared by studying large black binders that contained transcripts of other judicial appointees' hearings. The binders were provided by a division of the Department of Justice, the main mission of which is to shepherd the president's appointments to the federal courts through the confirmation process. When I was nominated, the division was headed by Eleanor D. ("Eldie") Acheson, the granddaughter of Dean Acheson, the secretary of state under President John F. Kennedy. Eldie was a Wellesley College classmate of Hillary Rodham and Francille Russan, the wife of my childhood friend Ernest Wilson. Fran ran unsuccessfully against Hillary Rodham for president of Wellesley's college government.

At the hearing, among other inquiries, I was asked about the latest decisions of the Supreme Court that had delineated when it was possible for the government to lawfully employ affirmative action, the constitutionality of the death penalty for juveniles convicted of murder, and whether I was aware of a decision of the Supreme Court that was decided incorrectly. These questions were not asked because the senators desired to hear my answers so that they could take them into consideration in assessing my qualifications. Rather, they were asked for the record so that the senators' constituencies would see that they had given a Clinton appointee a hard time during confirmation proceedings.

For the most part, the questioning by the senators was polite. However, John Ashcroft from Missouri was remarkably rude. He asked me what articulates the highest law of the land. This question was transpicuous. I knew he wanted to make the point that it was the Constitution of the United States that set forth the principles by which the country is governed and not the Supreme Court against which Republicans had railed for years.

Ashcroft was not pleased with my answer, which reflected my discernment of the political point he wished to make. I said, "Of course it is the Constitution of the United States that sets forth governing principles of federal law, but an issue only arises when there is a dispute as to what the Constitution means and undoubtedly it is the Supreme Court that determines the Constitution's meaning."

Ashcroft, visibly nonplussed by my answer, swiveled in his chair and turned his back to me.

The hearing went well. Only Ashcroft submitted written questions for me to answer after the hearing. The questions were juvenile: "Who was your favorite Supreme Court justice?" "What book or article most influenced your perspective on the law?" Doubtless these questions were framed for Ashcroft by his staff, but he was ultimately responsible for posing them. The Department of Justice returned my original answers to these questions as they clearly reflected my disrespect for them and the senator who had posed them.

My disrespect for Ashcroft was cemented when he became attorney general of the United States in 2002. He ordered that curtains be installed to block the view of the "Spirit of Justice" statue in the Robert F. Kennedy Department of Justice Building. The statute is of a woman wearing a toga-like dress with one breast revealed. Was this man unaware of the iconic partially nude female figures that Michelangelo had painted on the ceiling of the Sistine Chapel in the Vatican!!!?

On the roll call vote on the floor of the senate, I received yay votes from ninety-six senators—all who were in attendance to cast votes. I was sworn in as a United States District Judge on November 18, 1997.

One of my first high profile cases as a District Judge was one of the many proceedings involving Elián Gonzalez. Elizabeth Brotons Rodríguez drowned in November 1999 while attempting to leave Cuba with her six-year-old son, Elián, her boyfriend, and ten others in a small aluminum boat with a faulty engine. The boat sank, and Elián and two other survivors floated at sea in inner tubes until they were rescued by two fishermen who turned him over to the US Coast Guard who in turn delivered him to extended relatives living in Miami.

What followed was an intense struggle to keep Elián in the United States by his Miami relatives and the anti-Castro community in Miami's little Havana and an equally determined effort by Cuba to have him returned to his Cuban father. Attorney General Janet Reno ordered the return of Gonzalez to his father and set a deadline of April 13, 2000, but the Miami relatives defied the order. Lawyers for Gonzales's relatives filed an action in the United States District Court in the District of Columbia seeking to enjoin the INS from returning Elián to his father. I denied their request for an injunction. Negotiations between the INS and Elián's Miami relatives to retrieve Elián from the relatives went on for several days. The house in which Elián lived in Miami was surrounded by protesters as well as police. The relatives insisted on guarantees that they could live with the child and that Elián would not be returned to Cuba.

Negotiations carried on throughout several days and nights, but the relatives rejected all workable solutions. A Florida family court judge revoked Elián's great-uncle's temporary custody, clearing the way for him to be seized by INS agents. On April 20, Reno made the decision to remove Elián from the house and instructed law enforcement officials to determine the best time to obtain the boy. After being informed of the decision, Elián's Miami cousin said to a Justice Department community relations officer, "You think we just have cameras in the house? If people try to come in, they could be hurt."

In the predawn hours of Easter eve, Saturday, April 22, 2000, pursuant to an order issued by a federal magistrate, eight agents of the Border Patrol's elite BORTAC unit as part of an operation in which more than 130 INS personnel took part approached the house, knocked on the door, and identified themselves. When no one responded from within, they entered the house. Pepper spray and mace were employed against those outside the house who attempted to interfere with the seizure of Elián by INS Agents. Elián was returned to Cuba to the custody of his father.

Another extraordinarily challenging case was brought by the family members of seven Americans who were among the 170 people who perished when French Airlines UTA 772, flying from Chad to Paris, was destroyed by the detonation of a suitcase bomb in midair in the plane's cargo hold. This was one of the deadliest acts of terrorism in history but had remained overshadowed by the Lockerbie tragedy that took place ten months earlier.

The attack was ordered by Libyan dictator Omar Qaddafi and carried out by Libyan intelligence agents. The plaintiffs were reprsented by Stuart H. Newberger and Laurel Malson, highly regarded lawyers in the Crowell and Moring law firm. The case presented numerous issues of first impression and required me to understand the complicated investigation resulting in the identification of the terrorists who brought down UTA flight 772. It also required that I understand and then explain how the passengers onboard the flight suffered following the detonation of the bomb that brought down the airliner before they lost consciousness and died.

The *Pugh* case was unprecedented in that never before in any court had a foreign government charged with carrying out an act of terrorism actually appeared in the case and defended itself against the charges as did Libya. Libya was vigorously and ably represented by Arman Dabiri, an attorney of Armenian descent, who raised as many procedural and jurisdictional defenses as possible. Those defenses were considered and rejected after careful research. I found Libya responsible for the bombing.

More challenging than the legal issues presented by the case was determining the factual issue of whether there was a basis for awarding money damages for the pain and suffering of the victims who perished. Did they die immediately, and thus did not suffer any pain and, if not immediately, just how long did they likely remain conscious? What was the nature of the pain they suffered?

Normally when awarding damages for pain and suffering, there is no question but that pain and suffering had occurred, and the judge has a basis, however imprecise, for quantifying it. Most judges, for example, have been in accidents themselves and know what it means to suffer a broken bone, a pulled ligament, or a burn. But what of injuries sustained as result of the detonation of a bomb in the cargo area of a commercial airliner in flight thousands of miles above the earth?

To provide evidence of the pain and suffering of the victims, plaintiffs' lawyers called an expert witness to testify as to what the victims endured following the detonation of the bomb.

After considering this evidence, I concluded that the passengers aboard UTA Flight 772 likely remained conscious for several seconds after the bomb detonated and that those seconds were horrific. The victims likely experienced the plane's disassembling and tornado-force winds filling the cabin. For seconds, they likely experienced the scorching of their own skin and saw and heard the anguish of their fellow passengers as they experienced the same. Also, consider the psychological trauma of knowing beyond a shadow of a doubt that you will die a painful death and never see your loved ones, your children, grandchildren, or wife again.

For each second of time the victims experienced this pain and suffering, I awarded damages of $100,000; one hundred and eighty seconds equals $18 million for each of the seven victims. In addition, each immediate family member was awarded millions of dollars for their own loss, some reaching $10 million for the loss of a spouse or parent or child. The owners of the DC-10 were awarded $41 million.

I did not stop there. I decided that all of the plaintiffs' monetary awards were entitled to prejudgment interest, dating back to September 1989, when UTA Flight 72 blew up.

On September 11, 2001, I was driving to the US Courthouse when I heard on the radio that a plane had flown into one of the twin towers of the World Trade Center in New York City. At first, reporters supposed that a private plane had mistakenly gone off course and had hit the building. I listened to the confused reports of this tragedy until shortly after entering the court's parking lot when I heard that the World Trade Center had come under a terrorist attack. Shortly after taking the bench that morning, a lawyer who was speaking to me at a status hearing urgently asked to be excused because he had just learned that his daughter had been in one of the World Trade Center buildings that had been attacked. I adjourned court for the day and returned to my chambers to learn that the Pentagon had been struck by a commercial aircraft.

I went outside the courthouse and saw a scene that made my heart sank. In the distance, I saw smoke rising from the Pentagon and heard the wail of emergency sirens. I also saw military and law enforcement personnel surrounding the US Courthouse. They were carrying automatic weapons and wearing combat gear.

I immediately determined that I should be with my family and jumped into my car and headed out of the parking lot. I soon was enveloped by bumper-to-bumper traffic resulting from what amounted to an evacuation of downtown DC. I managed to drive back to the parking lot where I left my car and walked home along with one of my law clerks, Stuart Evans.

As it turns out, the attacks of 9/11 gave rise to the disputes and controversies that came to dominate my calendar for the major part of my time as a judge on the federal court. One of the first was a Freedom of Information Act (FOIA) action brought by organizations seeking documents pertinent to the president's war on terror program. The Freedom of Information Act (FOIA), 5 USC. § 552, is a federal law that allows for the full or partial disclosure of previously unreleased information and documents controlled by the United States government. The American Civil Liberties Union, among others, sought memoranda setting forth the administration's legal rationale for prosecuting the war.

The suit was met by the government's stubborn resistance to disclosure and presented extraordinary challenges. In resolving these suits, I had to determine whether copious documents or any portion of them were exempt from disclosure under nine exemptions contained in the law or by one of three special law enforcement record exclusions. One of the exemptions from disclosure was for documents that had been classified. Normally, determining whether any document or portion of it was exempt from disclosure entailed a rather straightforward analysis where the court employed the techniques normally employed to determine legal questions such as what other courts have done when confronting similar requests. The challenge for me in this case was that there had not been similar requests in the past for documents concerning the decision making leading to war that resulted in court decisions to review. Another challenge was that I was without the assistance of a law clerk who normally would have reviewed the documents and then researched the rationale put forward by the government for its position that the document was exempt from disclosure. In this suit, much of the information sought had been classified at a level higher than the security clearances possessed by my clerks. My clerks, thetefore, were not able to review the pertinent papers. It was left to me to review the documents and do the relevant research on my own. It did not matter that some of the documents clearly were overclassified as it indisputably is the sole prerogative of the executive branch to classify and at what level. That I was of the view that these documents, which contained only legal analysis, were not properly classified on the grounds that their release would jeopardize national security was absolutely of no moment. Consequently, in the end, I required disclosure of portions of only a few documents.

On September 14, 2001, Congress provided the president with the Authorization for Use of Military Force (AUMF), which enabled him to employ the United States Armed Forces against those responsible for the 9/11 terrorist attacks. This authorization granted him the authority to use all "necessary and appropriate force" against those whom he determined "planned, authorized, committed, or aided" the 9/11 attacks, or who harbored said persons or groups. Pursuant to the AUMF, President Bush unleashed the military might of the US Armed Forces against Al Qaeda, striking initially in the mountains of Afghanistan.

The effort to bring those responsible for the 9/11 attacks to justice included bombing parts of Afghanistan where Al Qaeda had its training camps and capturing those thought to be part of the terrorist network. One of those captured was Lakhdar Boumediene, a naturalized citizen of Bosnia and Herzegovina, who was held with other suspected members and supporters of Al Qaeda at the United States Naval Base at Guantanamo Bay, Cuba.

Guantanamo Bay is not a part of the United States, and under the terms of the 1903 lease between the United States and Cuba entered immediately after the Spanish American War, Cuba retains ultimate sovereignty over the territory. Arguing that the Constitution does not give aliens held by the United States in areas over which our government is not sovereign the right to test the legality of their detention by habeas corpus, the government argued successfully in the United States District Court and in the United Court of Appeals for the District of Columbia Circuit, that Boumediene's petition should be dismissed.

In *Boumediene v. Bush*, 553 US 723 (2008), the Supreme Court in a 5–4 decision disagreed, holding that the detainees in Guantanamo Bay had a right to habeas corpus review under the United States Constitution. Invoking *Marbury v. Madison* (1803), the Court concluded:

The Nation's basic charter cannot be contracted away like this. The Constitution grants Congress and the president the power to acquire, dispose of, and govern territory, not the power to decide when and where its terms apply. To hold that the political branches may switch the Constitution on or off at will would lead to a regime in which they, not this Court, say "what the law is."

While determining that a detainee held at Guantanamo Bay has a right to challenge the legality of his detention in court by seeking a writ of habeas corpus, the Supreme Court declined to anticipate and give guidance regarding the myriad thorny issues its decision raised for actually adjudicating these cases and expressly left it to the lower federal courts in the DC Circuit to do so.

Adjudicating the detainee habeas corpus cases present challenges that even other federal judges not called upon to handle them can imagine. For example, the protocol that US District judges in the District of Columbia developed for issuing written decisions in these cases is to submit them to the government before publicly publishing them so that intelligence agencies can review them and redact any portions of an opinion those agencies believe should not be disclosed in order to not reveal information that could harm national security. In one of my cases, I followed the protocol but within minutes before my decision was to be electronically published, my chambers received a frantic call from government attorneys indicating that redacting mistakes had been made by the reviewing intelligence agencies and asking that I not publish the opinion but return it for further review. I complied with this request, and after several days, I received the opinion with additional redactions. Literally within minutes of my filing the newly redacted decision, government attorneys again contacted me saying that again appropriate redactions had not been made and requested that I withdraw the opinion from the public docket. There was no precedent to guide me, and regrettably I granted the request and withdrew the opinion and substituted it with another one that contained further redactions.

My decision to comply with the government's request was the worst ruling I made in my thirty-five years as a judge. I should not have granted the government's request, which in effect doctored the public record—something that should never be done even at the behest of the government on national security grounds. At the very least, I should have required the government to show me why it had such concerns.

The judges on the United States District Court conscientiously adjudicate the Guantanamo detainees' habeas petitions in accordance with the holding of *Boumediene*. By necessity, these judges legislate from the bench, each judge devises her own procedures for addressing the unusual issues presented by these cases often relying on the protocol developed by Judge Thomas Hogan, a jurist who is unparalleled in his devotion to his craft.

While the judges of the United States District Court apply the law evenhandedly and without prejudging these cases, the United States

Court of Appeals for the District of Columbia Circuit, which review decisions on the detainees' petitions, does not. I predict that history will not be kind to the DC Circuit, a court that is second in importance only to the Supreme Court. The DC Circuit will be shown to have been a self-appointed battalion in the government's effort to defeat terrorism and, in doing so, abdicates its core responsibility to safeguard individual and constitutionally protected liberties.

The majority of the judges on the DC Circuit quite obviously disagree with the Supreme Court's ruling that the detainees at Guantanamo Bay have a constitutional right to access to the courts. While it is not unusual for lower court judges to disagree with precedent set by a higher court, even that set by the Supreme Court, it is very unusual and entirely wrong for lower court judges to refuse to follow controlling precedent, which the DC Circuit has done brazenly in the detainee cases. Many judges on the DC Circuit obviously put their thumb on the scales of justice and press hard. When reviewing detainee cases in which a United States District Judge rules that a detainee is entitled to be released, the DC Circuit almost never agrees, sides with the government well in excess of 95 percent of the time, and reverses the district court's decision on appeal. On the other hand, when the district court decides that a detainee is not entitled to be released, the DC Circuit sides with the government—again well in excess of 95 percent of the time—and affirms the decision.

The extremely high reversal rate of US District Court decisions in favor of release is astounding and simply cannot be reconciled with the proposition that the DC Circuit reviews these cases in an evenhanded and intellectually honest way, using the same standards it uses in reviewing other cases. The vast majority of district court cases, civil or criminal—somewhere far in excess 70 percent—are affirmed on appeal. The rate of affirmance for criminal cases—to which the habeas cases brought by the detainees are very similar—is even more pronounced. What accounts then for the difference in the rate of affirmance for these cases?

That the DC Circuit does not grant detainee cases an evenhanded and intellectually honest review is vividly shown in the case of Adnan Latif, a detainee who sought a writ of habeas corpus after being captured in December 2001 at the Pakistan-Afghanistan border as a result of a widespread dragnet.

Latif was brought to the United States Naval Base in Guantanamo Bay in January 2002. The US government alleged that Latif was a fighter and operative, that he went to Afghanistan for jihad, that he "took military or terrorist training in Afghanistan," and that he "fought for the Taliban." Further allegations were that his name or alias had been found "on material seized in raids on Al Qaeda safe houses and facilities" and that he served on the security detail of Osama Bin Laden.

Following a multiday trial that was closed to the public, I ordered Latif's release from detention. In my written ruling, I explained that the government had failed to show by a preponderance of the evidence, the governing standard, that he was part of Al Qaeda or an affiliated force. I found Latif's denial of the government's accusations plausible and that, at least as credible as the government charges was Latif's explanation that he was a mentally disturbed man who went to Afghanistan seeking medical care because he was too poor to pay for it elsewhere.

On appeal, the DC Circuit overturned my decision in a split decision. The majority decision was written by Judge Janice Rogers Brown, in which Judge Karen LeCraft Henderson concurred. Judge David Tatel wrote a dissenting opinion. The DC Circuit's failure to affirm my decision resulted in an injustice of the first order.

The DC Circuit's decision rested principally on its conclusion that I erred in making the factual determination that the government's key piece of evidence, a heavily redacted intelligence report, was not sufficiently reliable to justify Latif's detention. The DC Circuit determined that I should have found otherwise and have done as the government had requested, accord the government's evidence a "presumption of regularity." Its explanation as to why I should have done so is suspect to say the least—even to one who has no legal training.

Judge Brown oddly compared a highly redacted intelligence report, one without significant details such as even its author and how it was obtained, to a document submitted in connection with a tax return. As Judge Tatel points out in his dissent,

The logic underlying a presumption of regularity stems from the mundane fact that routine business is normally not fouled up. Cases applying factual presumptions have something in common: actions taken or documents produced within a process that is generally reliable because it is, for example, transparent, accessible, and often familiar. As a result, courts have no reason to question the output of such processes in any given case absent specific evidence of error.

A classic example of a proper presumption is that a properly addressed item of postage that is placed in the United States mail is received by the person to whom it is sent. As Judge Tatel states in his dissent, the report on which Latif's case hinged stands had none of the characteristics that underlie a proper presumption. It was produced in the fog of war by a clandestine method that nothing was known about. It was not familiar, transparent, or generally understood to be reliable. The intelligence report, was, in the DC Circuit's own words, and as I pointed out in my decision, "prepared in stressful and chaotic conditions, filtered through interpreters, subject to transcription errors, and heavily redacted for national security purposes."

It is clear to me and to other knowledgeable observers that the DC Circuit has succeeded in gutting *Boumediene*. Judge Brown, in her opinion in Latif, virtually confesses that this was intended. Judge Brown concludes her opinion in Latif with a broadside against *Boumediene* itself:

As the dissenters in [*Boumediene*] warned and as the amount of ink spilled in this single case attests, Boumediene's airy supposition have caused great difficulty for the Executive and the courts … Luckily, this is a shrinking category of cases. The ranks of Guantanamo detainees will not be replenished. Boumediene fundamentally altered the calculus of war, guaranteeing that the benefit of intelligence that might be gained— even from high-value detainees—is outweighed by the systemic cost of defending detention decisions … While the court in Boumediene expressed sensitivity to such concerns, it did not find them dispositive.

The dismissal, bordering on disrespect, of the Supreme Court's reasoning as "airy suppositions" is notable. This sort of criticism does not engender confidence that the DC Circuit is honoring—rather than subverting— binding precedent.

The DC Circuit's decision had tragic consequences for Latif. It meant that he would remain incarcerated in the hell to which he had been confined for ten years at the time of the hearing before me even though it had been determined multiple times by various panels that he should have been released. Both Joint Task Force Guantanamo and the Guantánamo Review Task Force that President Barack Obama set up when he came to office in 2009 cleared Latif for release before my review of his petition for a writ of habeas corpus.

The failure to release Latif and the conditions to which he was subjected at Guantanamo Bay should be of concern to anyone who believes that our nation should live up to the principles of justice that we frequently applaud—even for those who have attacked us. Remember Latif was not alleged to have done so. Rather, he was alleged to have been in transit to receive training by Al Qaeda. One of Latif's attorneys who was allowed to visit him in November 2004 reported:

During the three years in which [detainees] had been held in total isolation, they had been subjected repeatedly to stress positions, sleep deprivation, blaring music, and extremes of heat and cold during endless interrogations.

Latif also described to his attorney a visit to his cell by an Immediate Reaction Force team:

A half-dozen soldiers in body armor, carrying shields and batons, had forcibly extracted him from his cell. His offense: stepping over a line, painted on the floor of his cell, while his lunch was being passed through the food slot of his door. Suddenly the riot police came, he recounted. "No one in the cellblock knew who for. They closed all the windows except mine. A female soldier came in with a big can of pepper spray. Eventually I figured out they were coming for me. She sprayed me. I couldn't breathe. I fell down. I put a mattress over my head. I thought I was dying. They opened the door. I was lying on the bed but they were kicking and hitting me with the shields. They put my head in the toilet. They put me on a stretcher and carried me away."

Latif became a frequent hunger striker, and he described being force-fed as "like having a dagger shoved down your throat." According to the *Miami Herald*,

(Latif) would smear his excrement on himself, throw blood at his lawyers, and on at least one occasion was brought to meet his lawyer clad only in a padded green garment called a "suicide smock" held together by Velcro.

Latif committed suicide on September 8, 2012, at thirty-six years of age.

The Latif case is a stain on the justice system of the United States. In this and other detainee cases, the law was not upheld and reveals the dark underbelly of a system we would roundly and justly condemn were it to have failed to work to protect a similarly situated American. What would we say if one of our citizens seized and suspected of wrongdoing abroad was found entitled to release by tribunals that considered the evidence on at least three different occasions but instead he was confined for ten years and committed to a facility and subjected to such inhumane conditions that he decided to take his own life. What would we say had this happened not to Adnan Latin but to David Smith? In other words, what if Latif was not an "other," a Muslim, but instead looked and sounded like us? Would his God-given inalienable rights have been ignored as it was so clearly by the DC Circuit? This kind of refusal to recognize the humanity of people in the name of security, Manifest Destiny, and the natural order of things allowed for slavery, lynching, and all manner of cruelty and injustice to happen throughout history.

A case unrelated to 9/11 was one of my most fascinating. At about six o'clock on a wintry Friday afternoon—just as I was about to leave the courthouse to go home for the day—one of my law clerks, Andrew Chin, informed me that a request for a temporary restraining order had just been filed and needed my immediate attention.

A scientist was seeking to stop the dredging of sand in the Atlantic just off the coast of Port Lucie, Florida, by the Army Corps of Engineers, which was scheduled to begin the next day. The project was highly anticipated and had been in the planning for years to repair beach erosion in front of multimillion-dollar homes that had occurred as a result of hurricanes that periodically ravaged the coastline of southeast Florida. The problem was that the area that was to be dredged was the only place in the world known to be a habitat for a certain species of a one-cell bryozoan organism. The extinction of any organism is a matter of concern, of course, but the possible extinction of this one-cell organism was particularly problematic as it had been shown to produce a substance that showed promise as an effective medication for the treatment of some forms of cancer.

On the other side of the ledger was the fact that the dredging project had been eagerly anticipated for a lengthy period of time by the owners of the multimillion-dollar homes fronting the Port Lucie beach and had been scheduled so it would not interfere with the migration of a species of sea turtle that was on the Interior Department's endangered species list. Also, any delay would be financially significant: $75,000 per day.

I granted the request for a temporary restraining order as I was unconvinced that the Army Corps of Engineers was unable, as was argued in court, to get the sand it needed from another area other than the one that was the habitat for the bryozoan.

As it turns out, I was right. The parties settled their dispute the next day when the Army Corps of Engineers found another area to dredge for sand.

13 CHAPTER
POSTSCRIPT

The day I retired, November 11, 2011, was one of the saddest in my life. Though there had not been a spate of reversals of my decisions or a complaint made about how I was performing on the bench, I believed that the symptoms of my illness were impairing my performance, particularly the speed with which I was rendering my written decisions. I always subscribed to the thought that justice delayed is justice denied. I believed it was incumbent upon me to step down, a course my brother counseled as well. Nevertheless, to me, notwithstanding that I had served as a judge for thirty-five years, my retiring under these circumstances signified that I had failed. I felt that I had let many people down who had sacrificed for and respected me. This included my father and my daughters who were so proud of my being a judge. I recalled so well the day Alex had come to superior court with her first-grade class for a field trip. Referring to the holding cell in my courtroom, Alex proudly said to a classmate who had been giving her a hard time at school, "I told you that you better not mess with me. I told you my daddy has his own jail!"

After stepping down, I devoted virtually all of my energy to finding effective treatments for my illness. I first sought a second opinion from Johns Hopkins, an alternative course to going to the Mayo Clinic in Minneapolis, which had been recommended by Dr. Hoffman.

The psychiatrist at Johns Hopkins, a graduate of Princeton, agreed with the diagnosis I had been given years earlier, but unlike my other psychiatrists, he strongly recommended that I undergo electroconvulsive therapy (ECT), a treatment he thought I should have given the length of time I had been suffering and the intensity of my symptoms.

During ECT, which is done under general anesthesia, small electric currents are passed through the brain, intentionally triggering a brief seizure. ECT seems to cause changes in brain chemistry that can quickly reverse symptoms of depression. I rejected this treatment because of its well-known side effects, particularly memory loss. Moreover, I had seen patients being wheeled out of the rooms where ECT treatment was being administered who looked to be totally incapacitated, a condition I did not want to experience even if it was likely only temporary.

I also tried transcranial magnetic stimulation (TMS) at Sibley Hospital. For this treatment, the patient sits in a chair reminiscent of an electric chair employed to carry out executions for thirty to sixty minutes while an instrument that holds an electromagnetic coil is placed against the head near the area of the prefrontal cortex, the part of the brain that regulates mood. The coil emits magnetic pulses to this area, stimulating or activating natural electrical currents within the brain cells associated with mood, including anxiety and depression. The aim of TMS is to reset brain wave frequencies to "normal" levels, thereby alleviating symptoms of depression.

I tried this treatment twice, but both times, the device administering the magnetic pulses caused excruciating pain, like someone repeatedly striking my head with a wooden mallet. After the second attempt, I abandoned the treatment against the advice of Dr. Williams. He questioned the expertise of the psychiatrist who was administering the treatment. He wanted me to try the treatment again and recommended that I go to Johns Hopkins to have it done there. My experience at Sibley spooked me for good, however, and I declined to follow his advice.

Finally, I followed my psychiatrists' advice to resume playing tennis, not to compete, but to simply go on the court where I would do something that carried such pleasant memories for me. In the past, playing tennis seemed to have a beneficial effect and seemed to coincide with my emergence from depressive episodes. The thought was that playing tennis might have a therapeutic effect, even if I could not compete. I was very skeptical since the competition was what made tennis enjoyable for me.

I had stopped playing competitive tennis in 2002 not long after I had competed in the National Indoor Championships in Boise, Idaho. During a match in the third round of the tournament, I suddenly felt my right wrist go dead, weaken, and then start to hurt badly, something that had never happened before. I consulted with several orthopedic surgeons, including Dr. Thomas Graham at the Curtis Hand Institute in Baltimore Maryland. He told me that I had an aggravated condition of osteoarthritis in my right wrist, a condition that had worn away virtually all the cartilage there so that I was left with "bone on bone." This caused excruciating pain whenever I used it. There was a time when I could not open a jar or brush my teeth with my right hand. Regrettably, this condition, the doctors opined, would prevent me from ever playing tournament tennis again. I initially would not accept this prognosis, but I eventually did so after experiencing intense pain even when I hit the ball softly. I discontinued playing tennis for eight years.

Recalling the days of my youth, I started swimming purely for exercise. I joined the Water Wizards, a group of seniors who practiced at the Takoma Aquatic Center. I had seen an article about them in the *Washington Post Magazine* in which two brothers, each over ninety years old, were featured.

The Water Wizards are coached by Roger McCoy, an extraordinary inspirational coach who puts his senior swimmers through a rigorous training regimen. Several members of this group are quite good, and many of them practice daily, in addition to the Water Wizards practices on Monday, Wednesday, and Friday mornings. Most of the Wizards practice diligently in anticipation of competing each year in the DC Senior Olympics and the National Senior Olympics, which are held every other year.

The Water Wizards have a remarkable esprit de corps. The informal leader of the team is Lauretta Jenkins, a brash and intelligent woman who is very knowledgeable about DC politics and exudes confidence. Lauretta is a devoted and very good swimmer. She also is very kind and compassionate. One early morning, she saw me sitting at the edge of the pool at the Takoma Aquatic center and staring into the deep water. Sensing that something was wrong, she inquired whether I was all right. I told her about my depression and that that morning had been particularly difficult for me as I had had difficulty getting out of bed. Lauretta sat next to me and talked with me intelligently about depression. She told me of her friendship with John A. Wilson, one of DC's most effective politicians who had been chair of DC's city council for several years. Wilson took his life after struggling with depression for years. Lauretta was encouraging and urged me to continue seeking help for my illness.

After competing in several swim meets and achieving some success, I decided to try to play tennis again as Dr. Hoffman advised. Lucky for me, a neighbor and longtime friend, who is an avid tennis player, Donald Lipscomb, invited me to join his doubles group on Saturday mornings at the Aspen Hill Club in Silver Spring, Maryland. Donald and his son Darryl emphasized that the group was all about having fun. I started playing with this group fairly regularly and found that—although I was quite rusty—I could still hold my own. Moreover, each time I played, I became more and more comfortable and was able to engage in the trash-talking that was a hallmark of the group's activity. It was during the big-time trash-talking that I rediscovered my voice and ability to connect with people. Moreover, miraculously, I started to play without pain. Little by little, the strength in my wrist returned. With the ability to play pain-free tennis, the long nightmare of depression started to lift.

Crucial to my being able to prepare for competitive tennis was being given an honorary membership at the Edgemoor Club in Bethesda. I had belonged to the club for many years before I discontinued playing because of my wrist. My honorary membership was due to the efforts of Lynn Garland, the wife of Merrick Garland, a jurist of the first order whose appointment to the Supreme Court should have been confirmed but was not because the Republicans in the Senate would not act on President Obama's nomination. This was an altogether unconstitutional act that put to the lie the Republicans' frequently cited reverence for our constitutional system.

Speaking of which, I am hopeful that Republican leaders will one day soon find the courage to become statesmen and put country first to rid it of Donald Trump. It is absolutely clear—and these men and women know better than others—that this man is utterly unfit to be president of the United States. In addition to being an inveterate liar, an apologist for Nazi sympathizers and racists, and a sexual predator, he quite obviously is in the grip of a narcissistic disorder that makes him vulnerable to all manner of pressure by those who wish ill for this country. Observations by a historical figure, a remarkably perceptive observer of government, resonates in describing the clear and present danger represented by Donald Trump. Out of the mouth of Cicero, the Roman statesman, in 42 BC:

A nation can survive its fools, and even the ambitious. But it cannot survive treason from within. For the traitor appears not a traitor—he speaks in the accents familiar to his victims, and he appeals to the baseness that lies deep in the hearts of all men. He rots the soul of a nation—he works secretly and unknown in the night to undermine the pillars of a city—he infects the body politic so that it can no longer resist. A murderer is less to be feared.

I am comforted in knowing that Robert Mueller, a graduate of Princeton University—as was his father—is leading an investigation that will expose any wrongdoing in which Trump and/or his 2016 campaign engaged with respect to Russia. Robert Mueller appeared before me several times when I was an active judge on the district court, and each time, he demonstrated that he is an intelligent and hard-nosed prosecutor with impeccable character. Mueller is old school. When Mueller turns the screws on

Trump's underlings, I predict they will sing like birds to save their own craven skins.

My first tournament after an eight-year hiatus was the Men 65s Clay Court Championship at the New Orleans Lawn Tennis Club, the oldest tennis club in the country. I lost in the first round, but I had a most hilarious experience. In a most amusing way, it signaled that better days were ahead.

Security guard at the New Orleans Lawn Tennis Club.

When I arrived at the club, a portly black security guard indicated that the club's parking lot was full and directed me to park on the street. When I walked toward the club's entrance after parking on the street, the security guard said, "You don't look happy." I was taken aback by this comment particularly since I was at that time happier than I had been in many years. I responded, "You're wrong. I'm happy." He said, "No. You don't look happy, but I know what will make you happy. A young woman just ran butt naked past me down the street, and she is coming back. You stay right here." This brought on a belly laugh so deep that it hurt.

I next began to experience what researchers now call post-traumatic growth, a condition that follows and supplants the debilitating effects of post-traumatic stress. For me, it was recurring episodes of depression.

This growth results in the ability to discern much better than before what makes life worth living and putting the day-to-day challenges that life presents in proper perspective. I started enjoying reconnecting with friends and having lunch with one of them at least once a week. I now am much more revealing of myself, and I find that this prompts them to do the same.

I also acquired a dog. Princeton is a pure-bred Tibetan terrier whose grandfather won best in show at the prestigious Westminster Dog Show a few years ago.

Princeton

He is true to his breed. Tibetan terrier are indigenous to the Himalayan mountains in Tibet and were companion animals to Buddhist monks. Princeton does nothing more than provide companionship as his forebears did to the monks. To say that I am very attached to Princeton is quite the understatement. I take him with me wherever I go when I can. Family members tease me regarding my penchant for photographing him and sharing the photos with them and on Facebook.

I also have become interested in exotic sport cars. I now own a Mercedes AMG GT Roadster, a Bentley Continental GT Convertible, and a Ford GT Mustang. In addition, within the past five years, I have owned a Porsche 911 Carrera, and a Maserati Ghibli.

Al near the Hermitage hotel where we stayed in Monte Carlo,
Monaco, after attending the French Open in May 2016.

Al and I now winter in Naples, Florida, and I train every day in preparation for playing tournaments across the country and sometimes abroad.

I continue my involvement with the Washington Tennis and Education Foundation and the Robert "Whirlwind" Johnson Foundation where I am a member of the board of directors. The mission of the Robert "Whirlwind" Johnson Foundation is to restore the home and tennis court where Dr. Johnson operated the ATA junior development program that contributed to the development of so many young black tennis players, including Althea Gibson, Arthur Ashe, and yours truly.

Virtually every day, Al and I talk about how blessed we are. I thank God for our good fortune and will forever be appreciative of the foundation for this state of affairs that was provided by my mother and father and Al's parents, Henry and Emma Rucker

The end, for now, as life goes on, permitting me to have more memorable experiences.

ACKNOWLEDGMENTS

There are many people who encouraged me to write, taught me to write, made it possible to have memorable experiences to write about, and contributed to healing me so that I have the desire and wherewithal to write. This book, in large part, is an expression of appreciation to the people who have meant so much to me. I wish to thank them explicitly.

First, I thank my parents: Rachel and Henry Kennedy Sr. They were munificent people, particularly to their children, who successfully confronted personal and societal challenges and built a nurturing family in which Angela, Randy, and I could develop and thrive. They were effective first teachers, conveying to us important life lessons in the way such lessons are most effectively taught, by showing us how to live our lives by the way they lived theirs. One thing my siblings and I learned from them at an early age, perhaps the most important, is how to face challenges with courage and resolve in order to overcome improbable odds. Whether it be grief caused by the death of a loved one, illness, physical or mental, the overt racist threats of bigots, or subtle racism that is accompanied by a smile, there is only one way to proceed: Go forward with head high and confidence. Mom would often say, "Stay on your knees. Thank God when things are going good. Also, thank God when things are going bad. Things always could be worse."

We were imbued as well with the imperative that we conduct ourselves in such a way as to honor with our deeds and words those who went before us, fought the good fight, and on whose shoulders we have and now stand. A cornerstone of this obligation is when one falls, as each of us at some point inevitably do, she gets back to her feet and perseveres. Our forebears, while suffering lashings, discrimination, and indignities in many forms calculated to break their spirits, carried on and did so with remarkable good spirit and purpose. We must do the same. Failure is not an option. Further, it is absolutely required that we do for those who follow what was done for us. Mom also said, "Be nice to everyone. You never know who will be the last one to wipe your ass."

I thank my extended family, especially my first cousins, "the Spann Clan," lead by Chairman Gary Bell, BA, CPA, MBA, etc. Here, I think in particular of Dr. Clement Price, my mother's oldest sister's younger son, who was a historian and first-rate human being. His wife, Mary Sue, Rutgers University, the city of Newark, New Jersey, and this country, lost him too soon when he succumbed to a stroke that he suffered while he was delivering a lecture at Rutgers University where he was a revered tenured professor. I am sorry that he is not here to see the opening of the African American Museum of History and Culture to which he devoted so much time and effort in bringing to fruition. I regret that I did not take the opportunity to get to know him even better when he was alive. While I was aware that he was a well-regarded academician, historian, and spokesman for the city of Newark, to me, he was merely cousin Clem, always an engaged and enthusiastic attendee at family events who informed us of little-known historical facts pertinent to African Americans. It was only at his funeral that I learned of the depth and breadth of the respect in which he was held by so many people, persons of the caliber of the chancellor of Rutgers University, Taylor Branch, the author of a seminal book on the civil rights movement, the mayor of Newark, Senator Corey Booker, and his students.

I thank my other quite accomplished first cousins as well, James Price, a former nationally recognized elementary school administrator, Gary Bell, an accountant and former employee of the state of South Carolina who endures frequent teasing by members of our family regarding the many degrees he has, Veta Faison, a former well-regarded elementary schoolteacher, Jarmilla Price, a talented singer and fund raiser for good causes, and Dr. Thaddeus Bell an award winning physician in Charleston, South Carolina. Then there is Veta Faison, Aunt Lillian's daughter, a well-regarded retired elementary school teacher in Virginia Beach, Virginia, Jarmilla Price, Aunt Anna's daughter, a talented singer and fund-raiser for good causes, and Dr. Thaddeus Bell, a physician in Charleston. Thad does a great service in identifying the disparities in health care provided whites and African Americans in his online newsletter and blog "Closing the Gap." He has shown great courage and teaches by example how to grieve and continue living a joyful life as he has done following the tragic deaths of his son, Thad Jr, and daughter, Tonisha.

Thad was also a phenomenal athlete who twice won the world championship in the hundred-meter dash, earning him the moniker Black Flash in the Australian newspapers that covered the championships when they were held in Melbourne and Sydney.

My cousins have been supportive over the years in many ways. For example, when he learned of the severity of my depression, Thad offered to bring me to Charleston, where he practiced and taught, to be treated by psychiatrists in whom he had great confidence.

It is impossible to overstate the strength that has been provided me by the connective sinews of family.

I thank the ministers and members of Asbury Methodist Church, which was and is my spiritual home. Asbury was where my parents found spiritual sustenance for most of their lives and provided immeasurable solace during their final days on earth.

While my parents were my first teachers, I had many others who taught me well. I start with my second grade teacher at Carver elementary school, a segregated school in Columbia. I do not remember her name, but Dad called her "shake it and bake." He referred to her this way because of the way she tantalizingly swung her hips as she walked the halls of Carver in her high-heeled pumps. I thank Mrs. Allen and Mrs. Colston, my first white schoolteachers, Mrs. Allen at Turner Elementary and Mrs. Colston my sixth grade teacher at Whittier. She held high expectations for all of her students, black and white, and did not hamper any of us by having low expectations of what we were capable of learning and achieving, an impediment many African American students face.

Thank you, Mrs. Smith, my French teacher at Paul Junior High, and several teachers at Coolidge High School, including Mrs. Green Smith, Mrs. Helen Levinson, my history teachers, and Mrs. Lamberth who taught social studies.

Thank you, Professor Stanley Corngold, who more than anyone else is responsible for teaching me how to communicate in writing. I thank my other teachers at Princeton as well, including Burton Malkiel, James McPherson, Martin Duberman, James Doig, and Sir. W. Arthur Lewis. Thank you, Robert Goheen, Princeton's president when I was there. President Goheen was primarily responsible for truly integrating Princeton and making it a welcoming place for me and other students of color and women. Apparently, President Goheen's efforts in this regard were significantly influenced by his attendance at the March on Washington in August 1983 and Martin Luther King Jr.'s "I have a Dream" speech delivered from the steps of the Lincoln Memorial. I was there too— on the same steps. Because of the changes President Goheen instigated, Princeton is a much better university than it had been.

I thank my mentor at Harvard Law School, Walter Leonard, and teachers there, notably Lloyd Weinreb, Abram Chayes, Charles Dawson, and Archibald Cox.

I was extremely fortunate to have had tennis teachers and coaches who taught me the game without recompense. David Lifshultz was a godsend as he played with me shortly after I started playing tennis and gave me pointers for no other reason than he saw a youngster with potential who wanted to play and wanted to help him. The same is said about George Arner, a mensch of an individual who always rejoiced in the successes of others. I am forever indebted to Leonard Himes, my tennis coach at Coolidge High School, who took a real interest in his black players, exposed us to youngsters who could play much better than we could, and convinced us that we could play at that level too. Thank you to Dr. R. Walter Johnson for fathering the American Tennis Association's junior development program, accepting me into the program, and exposing me to a rigorous training regimen and high-level competition. Allie Ritzenberg, the tennis pro and coach at Saint Albans School for Boys, was important to Randy and me in providing us entree to the elite Saint Albans Tennis Club and Randy to the Saint Albans School for Boys.

I thank Donald and Daryl Lipscomb, Jim Hamilton, and Gary Wilson for their support when I came back to competitive tennis after being out of competition for eight years and having been told by multiple orthopedic specialists that I would not be able to play again due to the ravages of osteoarthritis in my right wrist. I will always be grateful to the members of the Edgemoor Club, my home club in Bethesda. I have spent countless hours there both before and after the condition of my wrist forced me out of competitive tennis for several years. I give special thanks to Lynn Garland who was primarily responsible for Edgemoor making me an honorary member when my inability to play tennis made it impractical to continue as a regular member of the club. Thanks to James Shephard, Edgemoor's former head pro who gave me superb (free) advice on how to better my game.

Important to my development as a tennis player and the enjoyment I derive from playing competitive tennis is the camaraderie of the many fine tennis players who share a passion for the game and who, tournament after tournament, give it their all, competing to rise in the rankings and for every point but never giving a thought to intentionally making a bad line call. So many competitors whom I count as friends come to mind, including the first players I identified as not only being superb tennis players but, more importantly, superb people with impeccable character. Here I think of Steve and Ramsay Potts, Harold Solomon, Les Nicholson, John Harris, Ray Benton, a Donald Dell, Ollen Dupree, and Sallie Elam. In the same high regard, I think of multiple gold ball winners: Bob Litwin, Brian Cheney, Michael Beautyman, Danny Waldman, Larry Turville, David Siverson, Neal Newman, Armstead

Neely, Phil Landauer, Fred Drilling, Padg Bolton, Hugh Thomson, Paul Wulf, and Joe Bachman.

I also think of journeymen players such as myself. We fantasize about playing the perfect tournament and winning a gold ball, the trophy given to the winner of a Category 1 national championship. Here I think of my friend and doubles partner Jim Feely, Michael Morganstern, John Curtin, Joe Touzin, Steve Duffel, Graeme Bush, Doug Brunner, David Wendt, Terrence Killen, Gary Jenkins, Mass Kimbal, Kevin O'Neil, Lange Johnson, Phil Lucas, Tommy Freeman, William Rogers, Winder Bill, Lee Adams, Lee Smith, George Deptula, Paul Shaw, John Davis, Dennis Postarero, Jack Ambrose, Wesley Jackson, Alan Geraci, Hugh Burris, Brant Bailey, Jared Florian, Marc Mazo, Francis Kreysa, Scott Wallace, Steve Duffel, John Reinhard, David Wendt, Dan Simos, Shippen Howe, John Tolle, Peter Briscoe, Howie Ames, James Clayton, Bobby Hampton, Kevin Dowdell, Steve Gottlieb, and Michael Daum, Jessie Pettaway, and Bob Royden.

I think as well of those players who have passed. I think particularly of George Arner, Ron Goldman, and Bill Muldoch, men who lost their battles with cancer but decisively won life's great match, living the days they were given with gusto and integrity.

I thank Haig Tufenk who organized tournaments principally at the Sixteenth and Kennedy Street courts in DC when I was a teenager. Because of Haig, youngsters were provided an outlet for their zest for organized tennis competition. I remember when my father tore down the draw for a tournament that Haig had prepared and hung it on the fence at Sixteenth and Kennedy because he thought Haig was favoring the Castillo brothers, Gus and Pancho, by giving them extra time to rest before playing Randy and me in the finals of a tournament. He was not, and I like to think Haig forgave Dad for his overexuberance in support of his sons. I also thank the volunteers who assist the tournament directors, including the roving umpires who handle the controversies between the competitors so very well.

I learned so much from my fellow students at Princeton. I am particularly indebted to Rick Webber, Kirk Unruh, Richard Howell, Michael Carrigan, Robert Bernstein, Paul Haaga, Stuart Taylor, Brent Henry, Reginald Penniston, Roderick Hamilton, Dean Buchanan, Paul Williams, Al Price, Jerome Davis, Matt Myers, John Mavros, John Vail, Gary Hoachlander, Michael Gage, and Len Brown.

Thank you to girlfriends who provided me affection and support when both were very much needed. Primary among these wonderful women is Betsy Paull, an intelligent woman who has character traits that I greatly admire. It is telling that she cared for her parents selflessly until their deaths with an uncommon degree of love and attentiveness. When tragedy struck her sister, moreover, she extended the same to her. Virginia "Ginger" Brown was impressive in many ways as was Jimille Shorter, Deborah Mitchell, Belkis Welde Georgis, and Gail Fields Jackson. Gail's generosity of spirit and Christian faith is so steadfast that it bolsters my own.

I thank my other friends in the metropolitan area of Washington who have befriended me over the years in different ways—but always in the true spirit of friendship. Robert "Links" O'Meally and Ernest "Chico" Wilson have moved away but have continued to nurture our friendship begun so long ago. The members of our supper club are great fun as are the members of Sigma Pi Phi, the "Boule," and the DePriest 15. These social clubs include within their memberships some of the brightest, most generous, and well-intentioned men I have ever known. Dr. Frank Spellman, a fellow member of all three clubs, is an extraordinarily caring friend as is his wife Beverly. When I was literally in the death grip of depression, Frank picked me up one Saturday morning in his vintage Mercedes and delivered some tough love. He listened patiently as I described the psychological pain that was searing my psyche. He then told me that I simply had to hold on and be the husband Al deserved. Ironically, Frank was the best man in Al's wedding to her first husband—and now he was being my best man too.

I thank George Haywood who persisted in his invitations to go to lunch even after I declined because I felt unworthy of his spending time with me because I felt I had nothing to bring to the table. I also thank George for his tips on nutrition and food supplements and the inspiration he provided as only one who has twice won the world championship in the 300 hurdles can.

I thank my former colleagues in the United States Attorneys Office who more than any others taught me how to try a case and argue an appeal. Here I think of Earl Silbert, Robert Shuker, Paul Friedman, John Evans, Johnathan Marks, Judith Hetherton, Andrea Hartnett, Mark Tuohey, Barry Levine, Johnathan Marks, Tom Queen, Vic Caputy, Steve Grafman, Carl Rauh, John Terry, Roger Adelman, and Gerry Treanor.

I thank the very fine prosecutors and defense attorneys I tried cases against and who appeared before me when I was judge. These lawyers were fierce advocates for their clients. The defense attorneys always conveyed that there was so much more to their clients than the conduct that allegedly brought them into the system and, in any event, that they were deserving of being accorded all the rights and consideration that are accorded those who are well-heeled. Here I think particularly of the lawyers who have worked for the District of Columbia Public Defender Service and the District of Columbia Federal Public Defender, including Tanya Chutkan, Sandra Leavitt, Michele Peterson, Jon Jeffress, A.J. Kramer, Angela Davis, Rhonda Winston, Robert Wilkins, Michele Roberts, Avis Buchannan, Rudy Acree, James Klein, and especially Charles Ogletree. These are simply superb criminal defense attorneys as are Francis D'Antuono, RonaldGoodbread, Pleasant Boadnax, David Schertler, Bernie Grimm, and Barry Coburn, attorneys in private practice.

I also thank members of the civil litigation bar, including Donald Temple, Jim Hamilton, Brian McDaniel, and the lawyers who represent the detainees at Guantanomo Bay, particularly David Remes.

I thank my judicial colleagues on the Superior Court of the District of Columbia and the United States District Court who day in and day out demonstrate why this country's civil and criminal justice systems are the envy of the world. Donald Trump's unjustified criticism of judges turns my stomach. I am comforted knowing that these men and women will rein in his excesses. These dutiful men and women are unflinching in their commitment to do the right thing for the right reason. I am especially indebted to my good friends and former colleagues Frederick Weisberg, Truman Morrison, Gladys Kessler, Paul Friedman, James Robertson, James Boasberg, Henry Greene, Richard Levi, Bruce Mencher, Anita Josey Herring, Kaye Christian, Ricardo Urbina, Reggie Walton, Ellen Huvelle, Emmet Sullivan, Tom Hogan, Amy Berman Jackson, Richard Leon, Beryl Howell, and Robert Wilkins.

When my mental illness overtook me, Royce Lamberth, the former chief judge of the United States District Court for the District of Columbia, met with Al and me several times and listened as Al explained what parts of my job I could and could not do. Royce was unbelievably sympathetic and empathetic, and he went the extra mile to make it possible for me to continue on the court. His efforts included taking some of my extremely complicated cases in midstream. I also thank my former colleagues who have passed on for their inspiration and example, including Harriett Taylor, Fred Ugast, William Benson Bryant, Lou Oberdorfer, Virginia Riley, H. Carl Moutrie II, Robert Scott, and Fred Ugast.

I thank my law clerks who over the years made me look good. I chose clerks well: Kaye Christian, Charles Davis, Paul Webber, IV, Kathleen Buffon, Marianne Niles, Elizabeth Karasick, Clarence Featherson, Faye Kagan, Deborah Pacheco, Johnnine Clark, Tracy Swann Price, Julie Adler, Ernest Rosemond, James Bresinicky, Carole Yanosfsky, Margaret

Watkins, Amanda Maisels, Lisa Harrison, Andrew Chin, Zoe Polsen, Ashok Ramani, Kwame Manley, Stuart Evans, Lexi Hazam, Richard Frankel, Cameron Arterton, Nora Engstrom, Melissa Felder, Lawrence Lee, Beverly Li, Ari Biernoff, Brigham Bowen, Rita Bosworth, John Fedele, Jeremy Barber, Brigham Bowen, Stephanie Brenowitz, Sean Arthurs, Nicole Pitman, Susannah Foster, Rachel Osterman, Sarah Marcus, Ryan Christian, Cameron Arterton, Nina Robertson, James Bickford, Rachel Cotton, Tobias Loss-Eaton, Shahira Ali.

I thank other members of my courthouse families, both at the superior court and the United States District Court. This includes my secretary, Faye Lyles, who became a friend to me and my family (among other things, she typed my sister's college applications), Bryant Johnson, my personal trainer, Angela Caesar, my courtroom clerks, especially Dottie Nathanson and Tanya Johnson, and my court reporters. I also thank the members of our superb US Probation Office, including Shari McCoy and Ganine Haggar who headed that office for much of the time when I was on the US District Court.

My gratitude extends as well to Deputy US Marshal Kirk Bowden and the other members of the United States Marshal Service. Several times when Kirk sensed I was struggling, he stopped by to see how I was doing and to encourage me. Kirk is old school in every way, including how he gives advice and support. I also thank a deputy United States marshal whose name I do not know who one day came to my chambers and urged me to carry on in the face of my challenges and to appreciate all that I had to offer.

I thank my new neighbors and friends at the Eagle Creek Golf and Country Club in Naples, Florida, where we now live in the winter and spring. Eagle Creek is a small, friendly, beautiful, and well-managed community. Its members have welcomed Al and me with open arms and have advised us about how best to navigate the paradise that is southwest Florida. This inludes Don Madalinski, the superb manager of the club, and his wonderful staff. Thank you to Chuck, Eagle Creek's world-class chef, and the superb wait staff who expertly serve up Chuck's culinary masterpieces. I thank Don Woodley and his dog, Jake; Walter and Jean Marvin, Bill Owens and his mother, Patty, Maureen and James Nowak and the guys who regularly play in the Eagle Creek club tournaments on Tuesdays and Thursdays.

Thank you, Brian Akers, Eagle Creek's tennis pro, for your encouragement and helpful coaching tips.

We have also been befriended by several Naples residents who do not live in Eagle Creek. They have been most kind and generous. I think here particularly of Lou Simpson and Kimberly Querry, whom we met through an introduction by our mutual friend Jamie Gorelick. Lou and Kimberly are remarkably generous. They are notable philanthropists, giving generously to Princeton, Northwestern, and Artis Naples. Al and I enjoy our dinners and lunches with them during which we marvel over the many people we know in common, many associated with Princeton.

We also have been befriended by Phil Landauer and his wife, Myke, master players and tennis coaches both.

We have spent time too with Charles and Reesa Reynolds, who were introduced to us by one of Al's Links sisters, Judith Batty, and Kathleen van Bergen, the executive director of Artis Naples, a superb live performance venue. Do yourself a favor and attend a performance at Artis Naples if you are ever in southwest Florida. Al and I saw Smokey Robinson deliver a superb performance there during which he belted out memorable rendition of old standards, including "Ooh Baby Baby," perhaps my favorite song of all time. Back in the day, brothers knew how to beg for forgiveness. Unfortunately, this admirable skill is becoming a lost art.

This brings me to my brother, sister, and wife, the three people who saved my life when I was in the abyss of depression by loving me day in and day out and encouraging me to keep things in proper perspective.

Randy, confronting his own disquiet, much of which stemmed from the tragic death in 2005 of his wife, Dr. Yvette Matory, would frequently write me notes using words he knew would profoundly resonate with me. These words inspired me and provided helpful instruction on how to prevail over my demons. One note reads:

> Dearest Hen,
>
> Carry on!
> Drop shot
> Lob
> under spin
> side spin
> Down the middle
> side to side
> underhand serve
> stall if necessary
> Day by day, hang in there until the momentum shifts
> Love,
> Rando

Another one reads,

> Dearest Hendo,
>
> More than anyone else, you have introduced me to the key activities and institutions that have shaped my life, Camp Atwater, swimming, tennis, Princeton, law. Thank you.
> I know that you're still hurting. I'm sorry. Sometimes hurting is just one's lot. But even with the hurting, you and me are lucky. We've got one another and much else besides. Remember that.
> I love you, Hendo. Endure. There is heroism in endurance.
> Ciao,
> Rando

There were more than one hundred such notes during my last episode of depression.

I thank my sister who supported me as well, all while raising her family and doing the heavy lifting in caring for our mother when she began to decline. Angela is a chip off the proverbial block, and she has the spunk of our parents. Angela provided me the unforgettable experience of attending a state dinner, President Obama's last, in honor of the prime minister of Italy, Matteo Renzi. I had the opportunity to say to him what so many people, and especially blacks, would like to say: "Thank you, Mr. President. You made us proud. You governed this country with uncommon skill while displaying an image to the world, one congruent with the truth, of a hardworking, intelligent black man thoroughly devoted to his wife and family, a devotion equal to that you have shown to this country." There was not a whiff of scandal professionally or personally during President Obama's presidency. I also said, "You will be missed."

President Obama acknowledged my words with his signature grace, simply saying, "Thank you." What a contrast to the current president, about whom no one would associate the words *dignity, grace,* or *honesty.*

At the state dinner, I had the pleasure of meeting, among others, the mayor of Columbia, South Carolina, and his wife and Jerry Seinfeld and his wife.

*Me with Jerry Seinfeld and his wife at the state
dinner for the prime minister of Italy.*

I thank my daughters, Morgan and Alexandra. When I was despairing about ever getting better and thought it would be better for all concerned were I dead, the very sight of Alex and Morgan put the lie to such a notion.

How could I let them down? What would Dad say? Alex was there when I began to sink into the abyss of my final depressive episode. Though not knowing what was going on with me, she held my hand and reassured me that I would be all right.

Morgan and Alexandra on Morgan's graduation day from Harvard Law.

Both Morgan and Alex have made me so proud. In the words of my mother, "I must have done something right."

In ways I am unable to explain, their accomplishments contributed to my cure. After all, what father would not feel gratified and made whole by a daughter like Morgan, who headed the *Daily Princetonian*, was recognized as a Shapiro scholar, graduated magna cum laude and Phi Beta Kappa, before going on to Harvard Law School and becoming a lawyer? Or another daughter, Alexandra, who rose to the rank of regimental commander to lead her high school's JROTC program; did well at Princeton, learning much and developing an interest in business as a member of *Business Today*; and then entered the world of business with great promise and effectiveness first at Under Armour and now at Twitter.

They both have made me proud in another way also. They have brought men into our family who are of the highest caliber. Morgan's husband, Tobias Loss Eaton, and Alex's husband, Peter Haviland-Eduah, are first-rate individuals, smart and engaged men with impeccable character.

Finally, I thank my wife, Altomease. For thirty-seven years, ours has been a romance and friendship in which love and support flows between us in waves without restraint or limit. When I was struck with mental illness early in our marriage, Al, day in and day out, loved me. She found my doctors, went to many of my therapy sessions, planned therapeutic vacations with no regard for the demands of her own work, and never gave any hint that she loved me less because of my disability. She also managed to find songs that expressed precisely how she felt and the resoluteness with which she would stick with me and help me battle my demons. One song was "I Won't Let Go" by Rascal Flatts.

Al

Sometimes when I was at work and was suffering the symptoms of depression, she would pick me up early and take me to dinner at TGI Fridays or Ruby Tuesday.

One time when I was in depression and was virtually mute, Al described interacting with me as like "clapping with one hand." Still, she did—and I heard the unmistakable sounds of her love.

Sincerely, thank you all from the bottom of my heart.

Printed in the United States
By Bookmasters